T0131777

SHEKNOWS.com.

THE
MOMMY
FILES

Secrets Every New Mom Should Know
(that no one else will tell you!)

JEN KLEIN

Foreword by Nancy J. Price *and* Betsy Bailey,
founding editors, SheKnows.com

New York London Toronto Sydney New Delhi

Adams Media
An Imprint of Simon & Schuster, Inc.
57 Littlefield Street
Avon, Massachusetts 02322

For information about special discounts for bulk purchases, please contact Simon & Schuster Special Sales at 1-866-506-1949 or business@simonandschuster.com.

The Simon & Schuster Speakers Bureau can bring authors to your live event. For more information or to book an event contact the Simon & Schuster Speakers Bureau at 1-866-248-3049 or visit our website at www.simonspeakers.com.

Manufactured in the United States of America

10 9 8 7 6 5 4 3 2 1

Library of Congress Cataloging-in-Publication Data has been applied for.

ISBN 978-1-60550-144-4

SheKnows.com Presents: The Mommy Files is intended as a reference volume only. In light of the complex, individual, and specific nature of health conditions, this book is not intended to replace professional medical advice. The ideas, procedures, and suggestions in this book are intended to supplement, not replace, the advice of a trained professional. Consult your physician before adopting the suggestions in this book, as well as about any condition that may require diagnosis or medical attention. The author, SheKnows.com, and publisher disclaim any liability arising directly or indirectly from the use of this book.

Many of the designations used by manufacturers and sellers to distinguish their products are claimed as trademarks. Where those designations appear in this book and Simon & Schuster, Inc., was aware of a trademark claim, the designations have been printed with initial capital letters.

This publication is designed to provide accurate and authoritative information with regard to the subject matter covered. It is sold with the understanding that the publisher is not engaged in rendering legal, accounting, or other professional advice. If legal advice or other expert assistance is required, the services of a competent professional person should be sought.

—From a Declaration of Principles jointly adopted by a Committee of the American Bar Association and a Committee of Publishers and Associations

CONTENTS

ACKNOWLEDGMENTS

This book starts with the March Moms, an Internet listserv I joined in September 1995. From that group I learned so much and made lasting friendships—for my children as well as myself. There I met Nancy and Betsy, founders of SheKnows.com, who took a chance on a fellow mom who did a little writing on the side. Thanks, guys. March Moms, individually and collectively over the years, contributed significantly to the thoughts and ideas in this book being well formed and not just the ramblings of an overtired mom in a caffeine-induced haze. Thank you all for your communal wisdom and support, for challenging me in my ideas about motherhood so I became a better mother, and for your buoying warmth at some very dark times over the years.

My sincere appreciation and thanks to the awesome moms who so freely gave sound bites of their own experiences: Katherine Adams, Kellie Bresnehan, Mary Lou Buell, Ruth DeFoster, Lauren Deichman, Hadass Eviatar, Kim Grundy, Polli Kenn, Jen Olsen, Victoria Palay, Jenn Petersen, Ellen Satter, Debby Stopp, Lynne Thompson, Michele Thompson, Angie Thorsell, Christine Van Dae, and Karen Wong. I wish that I could have used every last one of your quotes; they were all worthy and insightful.

Never underestimate the power of a cheering section and friends willing to read a rough draft! Those who gave support and encouragement are too many to name, but they include Lauren, my closest and oldest friend: I learn from you every day—you are the kind of mother I want to be when I grow up—Jen, Katherine, Polli, Michele, and Liz. Thank you.

Thanks to Andrea Zuckerman and Julian Huang for your input.

I could not have written a word of this book without the love and support of my husband, Andreas. He made coffee, read, critiqued, made emotional space for me to work, encouraged, supported, rubbed my back, and was generally the most awesome husband ever. He, of course, was my inspiration for Chapter 10. Thank you, sweetie.

Finally, my children: Aaron, Piers, and Greta. Thank you for enduring an often crabby and stressed-out mom while I tried to birth this book. The three of you are amazing beyond words and make me want to be a better mother, each and every day.

FOREWORD

Most parenting adventures start with a few simple words: "We're having a baby!" And while those words are factual, they tell so little of the real story they could almost be considered a lie.

You're not having a baby—not really. You're having a whole person, and you're embarking on one of the most exhilarating, exhausting, rewarding, frustrating, beautiful, messy, soothing, frenetic, profound, amusing, and altogether amazing experiences of your life.

And you're going in without a map.

But in so many ways, how lucky you are to be pregnant now. Starting our families in the early to mid-1990s, we experienced our first pregnancies in the pre–World Wide Web dark ages, before the incredible opportunity to connect with a diverse community of moms you can find online these days (and, sadly, before there were many decent maternity clothes).

Technology moves fast, however, and by our second pregnancies, we had the web at our fingertips. Meeting expectant moms (new and experienced) from all over the world, we suddenly had access to a lot more information about pregnancy, birth, and parenting than we realized existed. We discovered a greater depth of opportunities and possibilities than we ever found in the books our doctors passed out in their offices or between the glossy covers of the parenting magazines we flipped through in the waiting room.

We—Nancy and Betsy (and Jen, the author of this book!)—are three such moms who actually met each other on an online pregnancy e-mail discussion group. Transformed by our experience connecting with so many other moms, we were inspired by the sisterhood: the give and take; the rich advice; the thoughtful, meaningful discussions. With that wind in our sails, we set out to establish an all-new resource to empower other new and expectant moms in a similar way . . . and that ever-growing community thrives today at SheKnows.com and PregnancyAndBaby.com. We're excited to see that mission furthered through the publication of this book.

In parenting, perhaps more so than any other experience in your life, the journey is the destination. From the moment you embark on this adventure, you will encounter dozens of choices, sometimes an overwhelming array. This book is not only an information-rich tool to help you navigate the challenges of raising one or more little persons, but a reminder that you are not in this alone. The purpose of this book isn't to tell you how you should do anything. The goal is simply to offer some tools to help you make the best choices for you and your family, and ultimately, help you feel at peace with those decisions and the knowledge that you are doing the very best you can, like so many mothers who have gone before you. And take heart: Just the fact that you're reading this book—or any parenting book!—proves that you're one of the good ones.

Best wishes as you embark on this glorious journey,

Nancy J. Price and Betsy Bailey (each a mama of four children)
Founders and Executive Editors
SheKnows.com and PregnancyAndBaby.com

Holy Cow! The Test Turned Positive!

On a hot July night, my husband and I lay in bed, wide-awake. We were in shock. The morning alarm ticked closer and closer. Every few minutes, one of us would say to the other, shifting a little, "Are you still awake?" And then, "Oh, my God." The other would reply, "Yeah, I know."

That evening we had learned I was pregnant. It might not seem like it, but we were thrilled! We'd been trying to get pregnant for some time, yet were stunned to learn all the pieces worked. We wanted this, but we were also terrified. Our life would never be the same again, something I thought I knew would happen when we acted on our intention to start a family, but the enormity of the responsibility bore down on me. I thought I could hear the universe mock me.

If I could whisper a piece of advice to myself on that night, I'm not sure what it would be. My younger self could never comprehend the joys and challenges that were in store, the strength she'd have in hard situations and how weak she'd feel at the same time. She might imagine the heart-pounding thrill of meeting her child for the first time, but she wouldn't understand the power of that feeling, the animal-like protectiveness. Not yet. She wouldn't understand what it would mean to be so tired that the thought of crying wasn't enough, or the peace she'd feel that her baby was healthy and thriving and asleep in his bed. She just wouldn't understand.

Today, I understand that the secret to being a mom means trusting your inner voice. I go on instinct, mostly—and *lots* of love. From the many moms I've spoken with (on both the good days and the less-than-good days), we're all just figuring it out as we go. Acknowledged experts on child development give hypothetical advice for hypothetical situations, but when it comes to individual children and their individual parents and our fallible nature and all the variables that go into every interaction, no one has all the answers all the time. And anyone who claims they do? Turn the other way and run. Fast. But there are lessons to learn from the foibles and successes of moms just like you!

The title "Mom" is received instantaneously, as soon as a pregnancy test turns positive. It's not something earned, but a gift granted. Growing into the name, though, that takes time—well beyond the forty weeks of pregnancy. Years after first learning I was pregnant, after countless experiences—good and bad, mental and physical—I feel fortunate to be the mother of three amazing children. Every day, in little ways, I continue to grow into the title of Mom.

Maybe what my younger self needed to hear from my older self is this: You are going to figure it out, and it's going to be okay.

Part I
PREGNANCY

CHAPTER 1

Imagining the Possibilities

Suddenly, you have so much more to think about. During the first few weeks of a pregnancy, a door opens to an emotional part of your brain that you didn't even know existed. It's not just that you have the huge task of wrapping your head around the idea that you will be someone's mother. There is so much more to imagine, to consider, to fret over, to confound, to educate yourself about, and beyond . . . all in addition to living your "normal" life, which, by the way, keeps plugging along, day by day. The world stops for no pregnant woman.

Your Inner Play-by-Play Announcer

Like the news ticker at the bottom of the television screen, this new emotional life provides a running dialog underneath every moment, action, interaction, and even silence:

"I'm pregnant. Wow. Am I really pregnant? I don't feel pregnant. I don't look pregnant. Maybe the test was wrong. Should I take another one? Maybe I really am pregnant. My boobs sure are sore. And I am pretty gassy. I wonder if it's a boy or a girl. I wonder what the baby will look like. Will it have my eyes or my husband's nose? I hope it doesn't have my father's ears. Will it be musical? Will it be brainy? Will it be athletic? It's a girl, I'm sure of it. Will she be girly? Do I want her to be girly? Maybe I don't. I don't know. No, no, it's definitely a boy. I hope he's tall. Oh no, what if I don't stay pregnant? What if I have a miscarriage? I don't think I could bear that. Stop thinking like that. You're pregnant and you are going to have a baby in nine months. Or eight and a half. Or something like that. I wonder how big my belly will be. Will the rest of me get big, too? I'm going to eat very carefully and never stray from healthy, organic foods. I will eat perfectly. I will. I will, I will, I will. Do I have enough life insurance? College costs *how* much? Maybe an only child is fine. I wonder what the maternity leave policy is at work. I'm so tired. I wish I could lie down right now and take a nap."

Repeat, with slight variations, constantly for the foreseeable future. It's overwhelming, it's scary, it's pretty normal. It's also exciting, very exciting.

> *"Having a child is surely the most beautifully irrational*
> *act that two people in love can commit."*
> —Bill Cosby

The first few weeks of being pregnant are obviously just the beginning, but don't dismiss the reverie of them or push them aside too quickly because it's still "too early." They really are a time to let yourself dream and hope and fear. Soon enough, realities will intrude!

High Hopes . . .

The hopes you have for your child and for your own future, both as an individual and as a parent, may come into sharp focus as you see the outcome of the pregnancy test. Whether it's your hopes and plans becoming a little closer or more distant or the hopes you have for the life of your child, the possibility of what could come and what will come is much bigger than your belly will ever be, bigger than your life. Suddenly, you look beyond your own lifespan and into your child's. The whole world opens up before you for the life of your child—even as the door shuts quietly on your old life. You might not even hear the doorknob click.

SHEKNOWS SECRET: Let yourself hope for your child, whatever those hopes may be.

"My first pregnancy was unexpected. The doctor examined me, confirmed that I was pregnant, and sent me home with a book. The first line read, 'Congratulations. The life you have begun will most likely continue for the next seventy-four years.' That number hit me like a ton of bricks. Seventy-four years? What was I getting myself into?" —Mary Lou B.

Maybe your hope for your child is that she has the same kind of childhood you or your partner had, or something entirely different. Maybe your hopes for your child center around achievements or personal connections or on love of the world around them. Maybe your hope is simply that your child be happy and healthy. Hopes can be elaborate or simple. "I hope my child grows up to be able to pick up his own socks," is as valid a hope as, "I hope my child grows up to cure cancer." Maybe your hope is for what you can give to your child, whether it is wisdom or an inheritance. Create hopes for the life growing inside you, be they serious or silly. It's part of your emotional preparation for motherhood.

. . . and Deep Fears

Alongside the hopes for your child come fears. While many of us are under no delusion that the world around us is absolutely safe, it can suddenly feel exceedingly dangerous when you are pregnant. The ways in which you reduce and mitigate dangers and risks for yourself take on new meaning and urgency when you think about bringing a tiny child along for the ride. Maybe you're suddenly more careful about the speed limit or more aware of walking in the park alone at dusk.

As if that weren't enough, you may also have fears about the pregnancy itself. Fears of miscarriage are normal, as are fears of the baby's general health and your own. This conception thing is such an astonishing miracle: you are creating an entire, wholly unique person from just one egg and one sperm and only that specific egg and sperm could join to make this specific baby—a different egg and a different sperm would create a different baby. There's so much that can go wrong, yes, but there's so much that goes right.

SHEKNOWS SECRET: Yes, things can go wrong with the pregnancy—but remember that so much goes right most of the time.

Look around you then look in the mirror. Think of all the people you know, from infant to geriatric, for whom the journey from fertilized cell to birth went so right. Think of all the people who have survived and thrived even among all the dangers and risks in our crazy world, some achieving hopes and dreams beyond their imagining. Let them be your reassurance. It's not a promise that everything will be perfect, but it can help you tap into the better odds that yes, it will be alright. Talk about your feelings with your partner and with close friends and family; let them help reassure you, too.

SHEKNOWS HOW TO OVERCOME PREGNANCY BLAHS
If you ever feel tired of being pregnant or depressed about losing your former shape or overwhelmed and scared about all the changes yet to come, rest assured: The pregnancy blahs are perfectly normal! It's okay to feel this way, and no, it does not make you a bad mother. It's okay to acknowledge that pregnancy is a less-than-perfect state of being—it's no insult to your baby. To cope with your fears and stresses, take extra-special care of yourself. Get some exercise to help lift your mood; try some prenatal yoga or even simple deep-breathing exercises. Don't ever feel guilty about taking naps, and let it all out if you need to with a good cry.

For even more advice on this and other ways to take care of yourself, visit *http://PregnancyAndBaby.com/ pregnancy/Pregnancy-Health-and-Wellness-Self-care*.

Like many women, you might react to this roller coaster of hopes and fears and realizations and hormones by trying to hold on to control where you can. You might not be able to control the sudden inability to button your favorite pants, but you can start educating yourself about pregnancy and childbirth and early parenting while managing some of the practical details of this new phase of your life. It might not be quite the level of control you're used to, but it's a positive step toward managing this new emotional life.

Shattering the Illusion of Control

The roller coaster ride of hopes and fears every newly pregnant woman takes can make you feel out of control—especially when the ride goes to higher heights and lower lows with the addition of hormones. And you are out of control to a certain extent; this newly expanded emotional life is just a symptom of that greater realization. You may try to maintain the illusion of control, but it's just that, an illusion. This little creature growing deep in your abdomen, perhaps barely the size of a grain of rice, is wrestling it from you. Your body is not your own anymore! Physically, you are losing some control of your body; emotionally, you are also losing some control, as your brain embraces the work and worry of parenthood and reacts to pregnancy hormones; and practically, you are losing absolute control of the direction of your life. From here on out, it's about more than just you. Yes, you're losing some control, but that loss will be balanced out by milky sweet smells and chunky, edible thighs.

"I learned I was pregnant when I took a home pregnancy test. I bounded out of the bathroom, so choked up I could barely speak, but somehow I was able to tell my husband that the pregnancy test came out positive. The first thing my husband said was, 'Where are the instructions for the test?!'" —Jen O.

Ask for Help!

Some women have a tougher time managing the hormonal roller coaster than others. You may find that you need help managing these emotions. Particularly at times of big life transitions, and having a baby definitely qualifies, getting a little help figuring out what it means to you and strategizing coping skills is a very smart thing to do. I'll say it again many times throughout this book: Ask for help if you need it, whether from a friend, relative, colleague, or medical professional.

In the first weeks of my first pregnancy, amid excitement and trying to retain some control, I did what so many women do: I went to the bookstore and came home with a stack of books that were better measured in feet than inches. Then I brought home more from the library. I read voraciously—as long as I could stay awake, that is, in my first trimester exhaustion. It was both reassuring and overwhelming. Some books were awesome and some struck me as . . . odd, or just plain off. I kept what I liked and got rid of the rest and started to get my first true sense of what my approach to pregnancy and parenting might be. Mostly, it helped me get used to the idea of being pregnant by telling me what was happening in my body.

SHEKNOWS SECRET: Be very careful about the information you take from various websites; make sure the sources are reliable.

I looked to the Internet, too, for information. There, I found conflicting information that completely confused what I was reading in the books. I knew instinctively that I had to be very careful about the information I took from various sites; I had to make sure the sources were reliable. I had to be sure to separate valid data from anecdote. That was tough at times, but worth it.

What do "valid data" and "research" mean, anyway? Valid data comes from sources that have been reviewed by experts in science and/or medicine and is reproducible. Data published in scientific journals is rigorously reviewed; information published on websites of major medical institutions is also heavily reviewed (as much for liability issues as anything else). If what you are reading online can't cite sources, the information should be taken with a large grain of salt. If a source starts out, "Everyone knows . . . " or "Studies show . . . " but doesn't reference the studies, question that source—either literally by sending an e-mail and asking, "How do you 'know' this?"—or figuratively by considering it an anecdote and looking for harder data.

The Internet also helped me find a community of women who were all due about the same time I was, and that was a tremendous source of reassurance and support through my entire pregnancy and into the early years of parenthood. Check out sites such as SheKnows.com for a wealth of mom-to-mom encouragement and empathy through articles and forums.

Matters of Scheduling

Just when you start to get used to the idea of being pregnant, practical considerations of pregnant life and future parenthood start butting in. Even before morning sickness sets in and your normal waist says its last goodbye, there are some decisions to make and actions to take.

Before you call everyone in the family and tell them you are expecting, call your medical care provider. You need to get on your doctor or midwife's schedule and start the process of getting your pregnancy watched with trained eyes. Some medical care providers want to see you right away and some prefer to wait a few weeks. Some want you to get a pregnancy blood test and some trust the home tests. Some might suggest other early tests and some might not. These decisions depend on many factors—your doctor's style, your age and general health, your insurance coverage, and so on.

SHEKNOWS HOW TO CHOOSE A HEALTHCARE PROVIDER
When it's time to pick a pregnancy healthcare provider, how will you know when you've found a good fit? Ask about his thoughts on the things you consider most important, such as: prenatal testing (including ultrasounds); C-section/birth intervention rate (and the transfer rate if you're considering a homebirth midwife); who your backup caregiver will be. Also be sure to consider payment plans, office hours, location, availability of parking, and ease of accessibility (especially for the month or two when mounting a flight of stairs might as well be climbing Mt. Everest).

Here is an in-depth guide to choosing a healthcare provider: *http://PregnancyAndBaby.com/site-guide/steps/13.htm*.

In the first visits, in the early weeks, think about whether you want to go through the pregnancy and birth process with this person—and likely others in the practice. A strong relationship with your care provider—one of mutual respect—is essential given the many intimate aspects of pregnancy, and he can help boost your confidence and reassure you throughout the pregnancy in addition to giving medical care and guidance. You need to feel that your care provider is going to take you seriously and listen to you; your care provider needs to be sure you are going to take your self-care, and his advice, seriously. If you feel you need to make a change, the earlier the better so you can be sure you have an appropriately strong relationship with your provider months from now in the homestretch.

Making Your Big Announcement — Personally and Professionally

One of the most exciting parts of early pregnancy is telling everyone else. After keeping a juicy secret for a while, telling family and friends that you are expecting can be so much fun. Whether you tell your entire family by phone or e-mailed sonogram or in person, there's nothing like feeling the warmth and love that surrounds such an announcement.

When to Tell Everyone

First, you should consider when you want to tell people. I know you don't want to think about it (though you likely already have), but miscarriages do happen. It's horrible and hard and sad, and untelling people that you are pregnant is much, much harder than telling people you are pregnant.

SHEKNOWS SECRET: There isn't one right time to share your pregnancy news; use your own comfort zone.

Every woman has her own idea of how far along she will be before she tells the world. Anyone you tell before then should be someone you would want to know if the worst happened. Some women tell everyone right away, some wait until eight weeks, others wait until the end of the first trimester, and others wait still longer. Clearly, there is no one right time. Figure out what feels comfortable to you and your partner and go with it!

Breaking the News at Work

Thinking about when and who to tell at work adds another level of complexity to the announcement question. When it comes to work and being pregnant, there's what's right, what's the law, and then there's reality. Even though pregnancy-based discrimination is illegal, it happens far more often, both subtly and overtly, than you might realize. As such, it's essential to be extra careful about spreading the word at work. At a time when you are feeling hopeful and optimistic, and maybe even a little romantic about becoming a mother, this issue can dampen the mood.

If you have a workplace with supportive friends and coworkers, awesome; you are one of the lucky ones. While you should think twice about telling coworkers before telling your direct supervisor, the dynamic in your workplace may be very comfortable and accommodating enough for you to be open about your pregnancy early on. Only you can decide if this is the case for you.

If, however, you are unsure about how your workplace will respond, review your company's medical and personnel benefits as it relates to your pregnancy before you make your big announcement. Your organization should have this information readily available to all employees. If you have any questions, ask someone in human resources (who should keep your request confidential). You can also visit some of the numerous websites that discuss the legal implications of pregnancy and the workplace; keep a folder of the information you gather and its sources.

After you break the news, you'll get a response you expected or one you didn't. Some organizations are supportive of working expectant moms and some aren't. Some will see only the down-sides—that you will be out on medical and/or maternity leave for a certain amount of time, that your work will have to be distributed elsewhere, and oh, what a hassle that will be. Some will want to know immediately what kind of leave you will take, how long you will be out, when you will come back, whether you will be back. While it might be a good idea to have thought about this, be wary of making a commitment to any one plan too early; you just don't know how the pregnancy will go.

"I was teaching in a high school when I became pregnant and my fellow teachers could not have been more thrilled and helpful. I was treated with respect and dignity and lapped up every moment!"
—Kellie B.

Sadly, some organizations tolerate discrimination (both overt and covert) toward pregnant women, knowing how difficult it can be to prove such actions. You're often dealing with other people's personal prejudices based on false perceptions. You may be doing the same job you did before, meeting your goals and deadlines, but if someone in your workplace thinks pregnant women are slackers, this may have an upsetting effect on your work life (as if you didn't have enough to worry about!). Keeping up appearances, being visible in your successes and achievements, communicating well, and keeping track of everything can help counter this unfair situation. You're absolutely right that it's absolutely unfair, but sometimes the only thing you can do is not play into that unfortunate, misinformed stereotype.

Hold On to the Hope

The first weeks of pregnancy are exciting and scary. So much has changed, yet so much hasn't. You're leaping into an unknown world but you have no idea what direction it will take; you've already jumped but haven't landed yet. While there are myriad details to take care of, the most important thing is to be sure you are taking care of yourself. Your emotional and physical health during this time—and consequently, the health of your baby—take priority.

SHEKNOWS SECRET: There will be challenges ahead (so, so many of them), but for now, revel!

CHAPTER 2

Stretch Marks Are Forever

The goal of pregnancy is to deliver a new human into this world. But before that can happen, that little fetus spends the better part of nine months growing in its mother's body, expanding and contorting her torso, displacing other organs, causing discomfort and even pain at times, altering chemistry, and generally taking over. The baby sounds like it's a parasite, living off the host organism until it's ready to be released—and in some ways, it is (but in a good way).

What Happened to My Body?!

You could spend your entire pregnancy reading about all the ways in which a baby feeds off of and changes a mother's body for its own development. It's really amazing stuff, and it's all happening inside you. But you don't have to read a book to feel it happening. On an emotional level as well as a strictly physical level, your body and your body image are going to change with the pregnancy. Your emotional self will never be the same, and neither will your physical body.

"If pregnancy were a book, they would cut the last two chapters." —Nora Ephron

I don't know a single woman who hasn't felt at least a twinge of body-image issues during pregnancy. Even the most self-confident-in-her-own-skin, accepting-of-her-flaws woman can have moments of utter despair. We may talk a good game, look radiant in our pregnant glory, but the inner reality can be tougher. You knew your belly was going to grow, but do your thighs and butt have to grow that much, too?

On the other side, there are women who feel a tremendous freedom from their self-critical eye during pregnancy. Pregnancy is their time to let go, not worry about it, and just be happy. And while that sounds great, don't be fooled. Those women have body-image issues, too; they're just suspended for the short term of the pregnancy.

Whether you are of the pretty-darn-stressed variety or the letting-it-all-go variety, remember this: although there is more of it, it's still your body. It's still you.

SHEKNOWS SECRET: Your body may present some challenges throughout the pregnancy, but it's still you, inside and out.

Your doctor is going to go over all this with you, or you can read it in one of the classic pregnancy tomes. You'll learn what to do, what not to do, what to eat, what not to eat, what's okay, what's not, what's happening, and what won't happen—and with luck, how to feel good through all of it. It's all very general and good information. What will happen to you individually, however? You won't really know until it happens.

Morning Sickness: Not Just for Mornings

Early pregnancy nausea can be completely overwhelming, and compounded by the heightened sense of smell many women experience. While some women feel sick from the moment they get pregnant, for others the onset is delayed for a couple or more weeks. Some women feel awful with no actual vomiting.

> *"I had to take Zofran, the medication given to chemotherapy patients, in order to keep anything down."—Christine V.*

Some women do feel nauseous only in the morning; maybe they throw up once, get it all out of their system, and are fine for the rest of the day. Others feel sick all day long, and all night long, and run a real risk for dehydration and related complications. Some women have to visit the emergency room early in pregnancy for intravenous rehydration, and that level of sick is scary for everyone. Some women even experience nausea through the entire pregnancy.

SHEKNOWS SECRET: Morning sickness can occur in the morning . . . or at any other time of the day.

Morning sickness, as awful as it is, can become somewhat reassuring toward the end of the first trimester and beginning of the second trimester. I remember a day when I suddenly felt just fine. No nausea, no pregnancy symptoms at all, actually. I convinced myself that something was wrong. I completely freaked out. I wanted that morning sickness back as reassurance that my body was doing what it was supposed to be doing. Crazy?

Absolutely. Normal? Probably. There were those internal hopes and fears again.

SHEKNOWS HOW TO MANAGE MORNING SICKNESS

There are plenty of ways to try to manage major morning sickness. Finding what works for you will take some trial and error, and nothing may be perfect, but you *will* get through this part of early pregnancy. Here are a few ideas to try:

- Eat many small snacks throughout the day rather than three large meals.
- Nibble on some ginger or try ginger tea.
- Eat a little bit before even raising your head from the pillow in the morning.
- Munch on plain crackers and protein snacks (cheese, peanuts).
- Suck on hard candies.
- Eat salty foods (pretzels, pickles, crackers, chips).
- Take your prenatal vitamins at a different time of day.
- Try some gentle aromatherapy—lavender is considered especially soothing.
- Use acupressure wristbands that put pressure on specific spots on your wrists.
- Talk to your health care provider about supplements or injections of vitamins B_6 and B_{12}.

More tips for managing morning sickness are online at *http://PregnancyAndBaby.com/site-guide/steps/23.htm.*

A Different Kind of Dieting

Whether you had difficulty eating during the first trimester or not, the guidelines about what and how much to eat during pregnancy can be overwhelming—especially if your appetite is taking giant leaps all on its own. There are more than a couple of pregnancy meal plans out there that claim to be the perfect combination of nutrients and calories, and include all-organic and free-range and hormone-free items and possibly vegetables harvested during full moons while choirs sing inspirational music.

Moderation Is Best

These meal plans are great as goals, and can provide loads of inspiration for generally healthy eating; the thing is, they can be completely unrealistic and often not at all compatible with real life or real budgets. Any diet that chastises me for ingesting even a milligram of caffeine during the entire nine months is crazy. And come on, chocolate is a food group!

SHEKNOWS SECRET: Your pregnancy diet should be helping you make good choices, not making you feel guilty by setting unrealistic expectations.

When I said that babies are like little parasites inside you, taking what they need, I wasn't all that far off. When you are pregnant you may eat for two, but you are as much eating to replenish what the baby is taking from your body as providing straight nourishment for the two of you. The food you eat isn't just for providing nutrients for the appropriate growth and development of baby, it's so you have energy to manage the physical demands of the pregnancy yourself.

"I think the diets are a joke. Pregnancy is difficult enough without the spectacularly ridiculous food restrictions that some insist that pregnant women should follow, 'just in case.' Being forced to give up some of my favorite foods and food preparations . . . has been torture. I've worked some foods back into my diet . . . but it has not been without some guilt."
—Jenn P.

This is all to say that if you are having a normal, healthy pregnancy, you can eat healthy, delicious foods that will support you and your baby while not obsessing over every morsel. Maybe one day isn't perfect in the protein category, but over a couple or three days, if you are getting all the pieces you need, you can relax a little on the specifics. You probably already know the "good" foods and the "bad" foods; just try to stick with the good.

Special Situations

There are situations, however, where you do need to be more careful about day-to-day nutrient balance. Specific medical conditions (diabetes, for example) require much more specific attention to relative amounts of sugars in the diet, and others require other attentions. Those are situations that require a closer relationship with your medical care provider and possibly a nutritionist to be sure you are getting what you need.

When "Now" Isn't Soon Enough

One of the more amusing aspects of pregnancy is the cravings. While not everyone gets cravings (and not everyone wants pickles and ice cream), suddenly turning the car around because you need—NEED!—that prune pastry—NOW!—is not uncommon. In those moments, resistance is nearly futile. Just try to have one pastry instead of ten.

What did you crave while you were pregnant?

- "I craved frozen Mexican dinners." —JEN O.
- "I needed McDonald's chocolate shakes and often jalapeño poppers (no idea why)." —LYNNE T.
- "Chocolate-covered strawberries, but I couldn't eat them because I had gestational diabetes, so of course I wanted them all the more." —DEBBY S.

For some expectant moms, the cravings are protein based (beef, eggs, tofu); other women crave dairy (cheese, yogurt, ice cream); others yellow-orange fruits (peaches, mangoes); and still others briny foods (pickles). As long as the craving isn't obviously unhealthy (and some women really do crave clay and other substances, and need to speak with their medical provider about what kind of nutrient deficiency such cravings might indicate), there's a possibility that the item you are craving is serving a nutritional need. Are you craving protein? Calcium? Salts? You might want to look at your diet. Can you balance the cravings by adding this element to the rest of your meals?

The Dreaded Scale

Hand in hand with discussions of pregnancy diets is weight gain. In our weight- and size-obsessed culture, people (strangers, even!) often think nothing of asking how much weight a pregnant woman has gained, while they wouldn't dream of asking the same question of a nonpregnant woman. Aside from it being none of their business in the first place, your doctor or midwife is the only one with whom you can legitimately discuss appropriate weight gain. No one else.

SHEKNOWS SECRET: Your doctor or midwife is the only person with whom you should discuss appropriate weight gain.

Culturally and generationally, the ideas of appropriate pregnancy weight gain change. What is considered appropriate in Italy or France is not exactly the same as in North America. What our mothers and grandmothers were told was appropriate was different as well. This may make you think that what your doctor tells you doesn't matter, but that's not true either. Ongoing studies and ever-increasing understanding of nutrition lead medical professionals to suggest certain guidelines. So, unless your mother is a medical professional herself, your doctor or medical care provider is the one to talk to about this issue.

Just Worry about What's Right for You

Whether it's a source of pride or slight embarrassment or something in between, appropriate weight gain is highly individual. Your weight to begin with, body type, dietary considerations, and other medical factors all play into the "correct" weight gain for you. Some women may actually need to gain more weight than others; some might be better off gaining less. Just as with the rest of pregnancy, every woman does it differently, and it may even differ pregnancy to pregnancy.

SHEKNOWS SECRET: Do NOT look to popular culture to learn how much weight you should gain and where.

Do not, under the best of circumstances, look to popular culture for validation of your body during pregnancy. It is just not realistic. If popular culture presents a skewed view of the nonpregnant body—which it most certainly does—it presents an even more skewed view of the pregnant body. Famous actresses and models not only have completely different body types and circumstances from the rest of us, they have staff!

"I Gained **How** Much This Month?!"

Even with a healthy, realistic attitude about weight gain, appropriate eating, moderate exercise, and a relaxed doctor or midwife, there may be a few months when you are shocked at your regular checkup by a higher-than-expected weight gain. Shocked and totally deflated; it's so hard to accept that even if you eat a perfect diet during your pregnancy your thighs might still get huge.

If you are particularly stressed about weight, hide your scale at home and ask your medical care provider to weigh you so you can't see the number—and ask that she not tell you the number unless there's a real problem. This may help you put the focus on a healthy lifestyle rather than the number during pregnancy.

The Pregnancy Police on Patrol

As if your own internal dialog weren't challenging enough, people—people in general and specific people—make comments. Lots of comments. And mostly about things that are none of their business. Yes, some people really are judging you, and some are oblivious to their impropriety, but they are annoying and inappropriate comments nonetheless.

Amid my own experience with the pregnancy police, I have noticed that there's also a double-standard for pregnant women. It's as if, as soon as our bellies swell, we're supposed to be "nice" all the time and not stick up for ourselves in these situations—and in spite of the effect of so many changes happening in our bodies. How else to explain the genuine shock that ensues when a pregnant woman launches a wholly appropriate comeback to an obnoxious comment? And then it follows with more comments about how if we're so negative all the time, it will be bad for the baby. Give me a break!

Why do people feel the need to comment so much about every action of the pregnant woman? Though comments may take many forms, positive and negative, it's actually not that complicated, and, for the most part, it's not about you at all. No, really.

Perhaps you've heard that Don Herold quote, "Babies are such a nice way to start people." That's pretty much it. Pregnancy and babies are such a symbol of hope and faith in the future that some people can't help but make a comment, any comment. Here you are, the blooming fruit of the future, and they are supposed to stay quiet? Well, yes, often they should, but in reality? Not likely.

SHEKNOWS SECRET: For every negative comment about your size, you'll hear two about how great you look.

I sometimes like to think of having a child as the ultimate act of optimism, your declaration that in spite of the difficult things in the world, the world definitely should go on, and long after we are gone. That there's enough beautiful and good to counteract the hard and the bad. The comments people make are, for the most part, their way of buying into that optimism just as you have bought into it by deciding to bear new life. In this way, your baby bump—and your baby—becomes a part of the larger whole, a larger community, with the most random of people thinking they've got some say. The pregnancy police aren't thinking about you at all, and often not even about your baby in general. They are expressing their hope for the future of the world. Truly. It's not about you.

Expansion Plans

You might try to associate weight gain with how you show, but they're really not related. How much your pregnancy shows has more to do with the relative orientation of your uterus, your body type, and your size than anything else. If you're a tall woman with a uterus that tilts backward and it's your first pregnancy, it may take a little longer for others to be able to tell definitively that you are pregnant. Some women show sooner no matter what, while others show later. You know your body so well that you might think you are huge when others might think you're just a little bloated.

"I loved being pregnant because I felt like I could keep my baby safe. I was terrified of the idea of him being exposed to the world." —Jen O.

You'll eventually hear someone make a comment about how "well" (or not) you are carrying, and hopefully it's phrased as a compliment. Regardless, the idea of carrying well is such an irrelevant term—just carrying is carrying well! As with everything else, every woman's experience is a little different, and can be different with each pregnancy. Whether you look like you are hiding a basketball under your shirt or the weight is more evenly dispersed all over your body, you are carrying well.

You may also hear that how you carry reflects the baby's gender. For every adage you hear that carrying this way or that way means a boy or a girl, I bet I could produce a woman who disproves it. The only thing that the way you carry your pregnancy tells you is that is the way you are carrying the pregnancy. That's all.

The Dreaded Stretch Marks

I've been amazed at the efforts pregnant women take to try to prevent or reduce stretch marks. I myself bought into a regimen of highly emollient (and very pricey) cream rubbed on my belly twice a day. Everything looked pretty good, until the last few weeks of the pregnancy. But then one evening, in the mirror after a shower (and in spite of my regimen) I caught sight of these weird reddish-purple marks on the underside of my very large belly. I was stunned. I was devastated. I cried. I had developed stretch marks.

"Think of stretch marks as pregnancy service stripes."
—Joyce Armor

It was more than likely I was going to get stretch marks. My skin is prone to them; my whole family is prone to them. The tendency toward stretch marks is a genetic thing, and no amount of cocoa butter or other treatment will change that—barring not getting pregnant at all. If your mom developed stretch marks during pregnancy and your sisters developed stretch marks during pregnancy, you might want to be aware of them, too. And if your family has no history of stretch marks, please don't come after the rest of us claiming that if we'd just do this or that we wouldn't have them. It just doesn't work that way.

SHEKNOWS SECRET: It doesn't matter how much you paid for the special cream; the tendency toward stretch marks is genetic.

If you are prone to stretch marks, you can try every treatment in the world and probably not eliminate them. You may (may!) reduce them, but not completely prevent them. And once you have them, they are yours to stay. Yes, they are. You can try every postpregnancy treatment out there and you will still have them—unless you get a tummy tuck and have them surgically removed. But wait—there's still more bad news. Subsequent children do not reuse stretch marks; they each make their own new set.

SHEKNOWS SECRET: Stretch marks do diminish in appearance over time—and you may even wear a bikini again.

If I can offer a little good news, it's that stretch marks do fade over time. They are much like scars in that sense. And don't forget the sunscreen, which helps keep the very sensitive new tissue from burning. If you have them, try to look at your stretch marks with a little fondness. If you didn't have those, you wouldn't have your awesome kid.

Glowing? What?

I've often heard people say a pregnant woman glows. I've been trying to figure this one out for over a decade because I never did glow. I looked astoundingly tired and wrung out, but glowing? Some women, yes—not me. I had some patchy spots on my face from hyperpigmentation thanks to all these hormones coursing through my body, but no glowing to speak of. (Sadly, I've never been able to get rid of the hyperpigmentation, either.)

SHEKNOWS SECRET: While perhaps "glowing" is something to strive for, ignore it if it's an unreachable ideal for you.

But I suppose that some women do glow. I imagine a picture of a blissfully happy, relaxed, and confident pregnant woman with an almost heavenly aura around her. While I suppose it's something to strive for, if it's an unreachable ideal for you, just put it aside. Especially in the first trimester, I can't imagine any woman glowing while feeling like they are going to hurl at any given moment.

Don't Forget the Hormones!

The ups and downs of your body through pregnancy are also tied to those lovely substances called hormones. Your feelings about your changing body are very real, but sometimes they can seem exacerbated by the roller coaster of the hormones coursing through your body. A tiny bit of weight gain can cause a disproportionate response at times—to the point that there's an inner you that is completely logical and accepting that seems to be watching this other, hormonal outer you have a bit of a meltdown—two yous rolled up into one big, hormonal bundle of fun.

> *"There is little I enjoy about the process—among the four of them I have had most of the least desirable symptoms, including a too-horrible-to-name condition that had me wearing the female version of a jock strap. Just when I can't take it anymore, the movement begins, a lovely reminder that there is a little person sharing my body for a while—one who is very happy and content despite my aches and pains. The most amazing thing about my pregnancy ailments is that they disappear before I've even left the hospital upon the baby's birth." —Mary Lou B.*

Some around you may try to dismiss all your concerns and issues surrounding your body as "just" hormones, but it's not just hormones. Yes, hormones can play a part, and they certainly are handy for blame every now and again, but the base issues and fears are real and normal. You are not the first to go through them and certainly won't be the last.

CHAPTER 3

The Baby Is Coming (and It Doesn't Care What Color the Walls Are)

Oh, what a captive market expectant parents are. There's nothing like the capitalist system to roll up all the hopes and dreams and fears of the pregnant mom into tidy products available for purchase, often at a not-so-tidy price. Every day, new items are invented and marketed. Every day, someone declares one (or more) of these items an absolute necessity. But very few of them actually are.

It's Not the Stuff That's Important

Before you go running off to a baby registry to sign up for everything in sight—including some items you may never use or use only once—take a step back. Just as simple wedding receptions of yore bear little resemblance to the themed extravaganzas promoted to brides these days, what your mother and grandmother felt they "needed" for the baby and themselves is far different from what we say we need today. Yes, some of the stuff we have available to us sure makes things easier, but whether we need them is another matter. The bigger issue is, in your hormonal exuberance, how much of this consumerist culture will you buy into?

SHEKNOWS SECRET: The love you give your baby
is immensely more important than the quantity
or brand of gear you buy.

As with everything else, there's no one perfect answer for everyone. If you have the desire and resources to dive in head-first and buy it all, by all means, go for it. But if you have neither the desire nor the resources, not having the baby-wipe warmer is not going to alter the essential characteristics of your parenting. I may not be a friend of the pregnancy and baby industries after all this is over, but I can live with that; the truth is, you can go through nine months of pregnancy, bring a baby into this world, and care for it safely without buying a semitrailer worth of gear. No, really.

Need, Want, or Something in Between

Do you remember the kindergarten or first grade discussions about need versus want? What is a need? Food, clothing, and shelter of course are needs that we all have, and our children depend on us to provide these needs to them. What is a want? Well, certain types of food, clothing, and shelter can fall under the want category, too.

In the excitement of pregnancy, the lines can get blurred; it can be so easy to declare that all of it is necessary. Of course, we want the best for our children; of course, we want to give them everything. But the simple truth is that as long as the base needs of food, clothing, and shelter are being met, your little boy doesn't care that he's wearing a pink onesie, nor does your little girl care if the room where she sleeps is a fully color-coordinated nursery or a walk-in closet.

Tailored, Not Tented

The first need you may have during pregnancy is clothes for yourself. Your looser nonpregnant clothing may get you through several weeks or even the first trimester, but soon enough the buttons won't button and other areas are just too snug. Thankfully, maternity clothes have evolved dramatically over the last twenty-five years or so. Gone are the days of itchy plaid tents and over-the-belly everything meant to hide, hide, hide; in are the days of high fashion and looking great. Along with this new and improved style outlook for pregnant women comes new and improved opportunities to put your hard-earned resources toward items that will only be worn for a relatively short period of time. The impetus to spend, spend, spend is real—spend early, spend often.

"Thanks to newer maternity brands, I really liked my maternity clothes. I think it had to do with that lack of self-consciousness. My favorite was probably a black, slinky cocktail dress that a friend gave me. It just felt great." —Lauren D.

How to Avoid Spending a Fortune

Unless you are in a professional or volunteer role that has a high wardrobe requirement anyway, spending a small fortune on maternity clothes shouldn't be necessary; you can look and feel good on a whole lot less. Between regular styles that are a little loose or a size or two up from your normal size and a few well-chosen maternity pieces—including items by well-known maternity designers specifically for the big-box stores—you can look decidedly nontented and definitely attractive without breaking the bank.

SHEKNOWS SECRET: With the wealth of fashionable options at low-cost stores, you certainly don't have to spend a fortune on maternity clothes.

If you have a group of friends who are fairly similar in size and style, starting a maternity-clothing cooperative can be a great way to dress well without going into debt. It makes it a little easier to spend on a couple of better items knowing your friends will likely use them, you'll get the benefit of your friends' similar investments, and maybe even see all the items again during a subsequent pregnancy. Likewise, thrift and consignment stores often have great deals on barely worn maternity items.

This isn't to say one or two great (read: more expensive) maternity pieces aren't appropriate. If you live in jeans, those designer maternity jeans might just be a need for you. The need to feel attractive is real, too, especially later in pregnancy when the reality of the experience is a little, um, fuller than you might have realized it would be. And if you plan to have more children, good basics that will be useful in subsequent pregnancies may be worth it.

Stuff, Stuff, and More Stuff for Baby

As for what the baby needs—and the baby needs more than just clothing—the prebirth buying and registry spree is only the beginning of the "stuff" years. Truly, the amount of stuff available for you to spend money on over the first few years of your child's life is astounding. While all of it comes with good intentions, and some of it really is very handy and exceedingly well designed, you need very little of it. You need even less of it when the baby comes home; much can be acquired over time when you learn what your child likes and dislikes and what makes the most sense for your situation.

SHEKNOWS MATERNITY CLOTHES ON A BUDGET

You don't need to spend a fortune on maternity clothes! First, you can get many of your basic, everyday clothes from consignment and resale shops. And budget department stores like Target and Kohl's have decent-quality maternity wear for reasonable prices. What should you invest in? Definitely make a comfortable, well-fitting pair of maternity jeans a top priority. Some styles are made to fit well from the time you have the subtlest little bump right through the end of pregnancy and into postpartum. You may also want a nicer dress for special occasions. And while you can make do very nicely with nonmaternity bikini underwear for the duration of your pregnancy, you will need to update your bras, perhaps even more than once during your pregnancy (by the end of your pregnancy you might consider wearing a nursing bra that you can continue to use after your baby is born).

For a lot more maternity fashion advice, please visit *www.PregnancyFashion.com.*

Making Do on Less

As it turns out, babies themselves, especially new ones, take up far less space than all their stuff. I've known families that have started in studio apartments that were just as happy as families with the four-bedroom Colonial and a large backyard at the time the baby was born. The baby won't even notice, and definitely won't mention anything. Trust me on that one. And if you do go for the big nursery makeover and don't quite get it done? The baby won't care about or comment on that one, either.

What piece of baby gear did you never use?

- "A Pack 'n Play—it just took up space until after the third we gave it away to a relative." —KELLIE B.
- "Changing table! It was upstairs, and I didn't go up there to change diapers." —LYNNE T.
- "The crib was a complete waste of space. We called it the $400 laundry basket. We're cosleepers." —HADASS E.
- "Never used that Bumbo—his thighs were too fat!" —LAUREN D.

SHEKNOWS SECRET: The baby doesn't care whether you bring him home to a mansion or a cabin in the woods.

What You DO Need

Babies and small children do have some additional needs beyond the simple food, clothing, and shelter requirement; babies need to be able to sleep safely and travel safely. And most of all, you do need to be sure that what you do acquire for the baby is safe. This is where a bit of research comes into play.

"I have not purchased much baby gear yet. A crib, a hat, a shawl to use while nursing, some art for the walls. I'm waiting to see what I get at the baby shower to determine what gaps I need to fill."
—Jenn P.

There are numerous resources for choosing this car seat or that one, which crib or bassinet seems to be the most comfortable, and so on, including many excellent Internet-based research sites (see the Appendix on page 205).

SHEKNOWS NEWBORN ESSENTIALS

For that first week home with your baby, you actually need very little! The bare minimum: a car seat, somewhere safe for baby to sleep, any necessary basic feeding supplies, diapers (with a newborn, you can expect at least ten diaper changes per day), and about a dozen super-soft, easily washable outfits. Not as essential but very helpful with a newborn: burp cloths, receiving blankets and/or a swaddler, and a sling or wrap baby carrier. Find more articles and tools to help you prepare for baby at *http://PregnancyAndBaby.com/pregnancy/Baby-Checklists*.

Baby on a Budget

Like borrowing maternity clothes or shopping at thrift stores, if there are some short-term items you think would be handy, try acquiring them preowned. If you then find that the item is a need for you going forward, then you can buy a new one if necessary. Not all babies, for example, like mechanical swings. I was so glad I borrowed a swing instead of buying one, even though several girl-friends swore they were a necessity and I should spring for the top-of-the-line model because I'd be using it so much; my son never took to it.

"I didn't think I'd buy as much with my second child, since you don't necessarily need as much, but the second time around it turns out we have more. Things become a 'must have' if it relates to convenience and ease of use." —Angie T.

Safety First!

When you think about borrowing or buying items used, don't look past recent safety guidelines! The idea of your daughter using the same crib you did is so romantic, but the guidelines about the distances between slats on the sides of cribs have changed so much in thirty years, and "I used it when I was a baby and I am fine" is little consolation if your child is injured by unsafe equipment. Safety guidelines have changed for good reasons, and you don't want your child to be a statistic. In fact, most adjustments to safety guidelines were made in response to accidents and injuries on older equipment.

SHEKNOWS SECRET: Visit *http://cpsc.gov* for up-to-date, easily searchable information on recall information on baby products.

The Fun Side

All of the do's and don'ts aside, baby shopping is fun! It's your hope for your baby in a tangible and extremely adorable form. Whole stores, brick and mortar and online, have sprung up to cater to just this cute factor.

> *"If you want your children to turn out well, spend twice as much time with them as you think you should and half the amount of money."*
> —Esther Selsdon

Some stores specialize in baby and child travel gear (the stroller options are just amazing!); some only carry items with a modern design aesthetic (think minimalist mobiles and sleek anything); some sell only safety-related items (you never knew antislip stickers for the tub could be so cute); some specialize in environmentally friendly products (organic everything); and some specialize in really cute clothes from frilly to ironic. Obviously, those items are more for you than the baby. While you clearly don't need most of this stuff, allowing yourself an indulgence or two if your budget allows is reasonable.

Making the Most of Baby Showers

If you expect to have a baby shower, take this great opportunity to get some of your wants as well as the needs. Whoever is hosting the shower may be able to offer advice to attendees about priorities and dreams when it comes to your baby preparations, or can point them to your registry at one of the major national chains. Your family and friends may not take care of all of your needs at such an event, but you can be confident that some wants will be addressed.

> *"We bought way too much. It's so easy to get caught up in the excitement of it and buy everything!"*
> —*Lynne T.*

At the same time, what gifts friends and family choose to give at a baby shower are their choice, and they often want to give items that have an "Aw!" factor during the opening as much as a practical side. If two items on your registry are the same price, you're more likely to see the bumper and crib skirt as a gift than the waterproof mattress pad. Cousin Bertha's gift of ruffle-butt tights for your daughter may not be your outdoorsy speed, but she gave them with love. After a warm thank-you note, it's perfectly okay to return and/or exchange them so you can take care of all the needs.

Emotional Preparation Versus Material Preparation

The pressure of consumerism during pregnancy and early childhood does serve one interesting purpose (and does it extremely well): distraction from the more difficult and less straightforward task of preparing emotionally for this big life change. Whether one can ever be truly ready for such an unknown journey is debatable; how to prepare emotionally can be even less certain. Focusing on more tangible things such as crib sets and bouncy chairs can even feel like emotional preparation in lieu of a clear path. And it's instant gratification, too! You get to take the stuff home right away, but you still have to wait weeks or months to take the baby home.

SHEKNOWS SECRET: Spend as much time trying to prepare yourself emotionally as you do preparing your home materialistically.

If you don't buy into the whole pregnancy and baby-products industry, you are not doing your child a disservice. Preparing your home for the arrival of a new little one is just the beginning of the many decisions you will be making as a parent, and going forward, the decisions get a lot more difficult than which stuff to get. With so many bigger issues, don't sweat the nursery décor; your baby won't notice, anyway.

CHAPTER 4

Writing a Birth Plan

The weeks of your pregnancy tick by: Six weeks, eight, ten, the end of the first trimester . . . the end of the second trimester . . . thirty weeks, thirty-two weeks. The baby is getting stronger and stronger; your belly is getting bigger and bigger.

There's this one event that looms large on the horizon as the weeks tick by, a light at the end of the tunnel, literally—for the baby, anyway—the actual birth. You know, when that little baby suddenly seems like it's going to be an elephant squeezing through a tiny keyhole. More than a few women have trembled with fear over the prospect of going through labor and delivery. Even if you look to all of human and mammalian history to reassure you of your likely success in this endeavor, it's still easy to be utterly terrified. Terrified of the pain, of the process—terrified of the unknown, really. Writing a birth plan can help you feel in control when so much of the situation feels out of your control.

Thinking about Your Labor

Before you consider a birth plan, it's a good idea to think in very general terms of how and where you want to labor. Do you want to labor in a hospital? In a birthing center? In a tub? At home?

Do you have some other vision? Early on in your pregnancy, your medical care provider will talk to you about birth options and/or give you some reading material about the options available to pregnant women at a particular facility.

SHEKNOWS SECRET: `Every woman labors differently, and every birth is different.`

No matter what kind of center you and your provider are associated with, there are protocols meant to provide a framework of safety for you and your baby. Whether you think you agree with those protocols is a decision only you can make, and it must be based on valid data and research.

Options Aplenty

There are so many different options available for birth. Provided you have a healthy, complication-free pregnancy, you have many possibilities from which to choose. You also have the choice not to make any big choices and follow what the doctor suggests; the path of least resistance is a choice, too. You still get a baby at the other end whether you have the baby in the hospital, at home, in a birthing center, or in the back seat of your car on the side of the highway.

What Others Say

Just as with other aspects of your pregnancy, there are people around you with opinions on what you should do and how you should do it, and a few of those people are going to think you are crazy if you don't do it how they would do it. It's really wonderful that these women had such a positive birth experience, whatever it may have been. It's great that they want to share their experiences. But there's a fine line between sharing an experience and becoming a bully about it (and they probably don't realize they are crossing that line). If at all possible, ignore them. It doesn't mean you should do it their way or you shouldn't do it their way; it just means it's not their decision.

SHEKNOWS HOW TO PLAN A NATURAL BIRTH

If an epidural isn't part of your birth plan, various other birthing options and tools for pain management may be preferable to you. Some alternatives to research include:

- **Hypnobirthing:** Wherever you choose to birth, consider a course in self-hypnosis and relaxation techniques to manage labor pain.
- **Doula:** Use of a doula—a labor support person who aids in comfort during childbirth—statistically reduces the duration of labor; use of pain-relief medications; and need for other medical intervention, including cesarean.
- **Birth center:** Attended by midwives, a birth center has a more home-like, family friendly environment for low-risk moms. Usually there is more opportunity to walk around and eat during labor, as well as laboring and birthing in water.
- **Waterbirth:** Relaxing in a tub of deep water can offer so much pain relief it is known colloquially as "the midwife's epidural." It also offers a peaceful transition for baby from womb to world.

- **Homebirth:** Birth often progresses most effectively when mama feels safe and comfortable—and for some low-risk women, that is in their own home with a midwife.

Get more information on these and other natural childbirth topics at *http://PregnancyAndBaby.com/pregnancy/ Pregnancy-Birth-Natural-Childbirth.*

Where to Start

Crafting a birth plan is one way to alert your caregivers to how you would like to approach certain aspects of your labor and birth experience. While many aspects of the actual birth will be out of your control, the birth plan can still be a vehicle for you to say you would like a certain response for a general set of circumstances. Of course, writing a birth plan is entirely optional—you could also simply go with the flow or have an informal conversation about your plans at one of your last checkups.

It's Up to You!

The decision about your birth plan is yours. You have to do the research, you have to do the questioning, and you have to do the thinking. Listen to your instincts about how you think you will feel comfortable giving birth, investigate it, and work with your care provider to make a plan. And then think honestly and completely about a backup plan. The thing about preparing for the birth is that you don't really know how it's going to go until you are right in the middle of it. You can plan and anticipate, but it's not something you can know in advance.

Research Versus Anecdotes

Just as you had to separate real data from anecdote in learning about pregnancy and fetal growth, you also need to make that distinction when thinking about a birth plan.

While medicine is not an exact science, it is built on centuries of scientific observation and research; a layering of knowledge on top of knowledge. While modern interventions aren't always perfect, they do allow many more babies to be born healthy to healthy moms. This doesn't mean that any given intervention is fool-proof, but it does mean you likely have options if you need them. While you don't necessarily need all the modern interventions and assistances, neither should you dismiss them outright.

"With my oldest, I'd never heard of a birth plan. I just assumed I'd have her whatever way worked best. I ended up with a C-section; I feel I was so uninformed about what was going on, I had no other choice in the matter." —Debby S.

What does that mean to you, practically? It means you need to, at the very least, understand the difference between hard data and an anecdote as it pertains to labor and birth. Your college roommate's story about her son's birth is an anecdote with lots of context, not valid data and research. The story may give you ideas about how you might like the experience to go and a direction to take your reading and thinking and research, but that's about it. Just because you read it on the Internet on a blog or a cousin's friend's sister had this or that experience doesn't mean it's an appropriate foundation for your decision. However, it can be something you should give more time and research to through validated sources.

For example, there's been much discussion in recent years about the rate of cesarean births in North America. You may even look at the cesarean section rate at the hospital where you are thinking about giving birth as part of your decision-making process. Yes, a hospital's cesarean rate is straight data, but gives little to no context about it. You can ask questions that can give you more context, such as:

- Does the hospital treat a higher percentage of high-risk pregnancies than other hospitals in the region?
- What is the cesarean rate for high-risk pregnancies?
- What was the cesarean rate among otherwise uncomplicated pregnancies?
- How many of those are complications from inductions, whether elective or medically necessary?
- What is the rate of successful VBAC at the hospital?

These kinds of questions yield answers that can give you a more solid foundation for your decision making or help you form more questions about why the cesarean rate at a particular hospital is high for otherwise uncomplicated pregnancies, and give you ideas about elements of your birth plan that may help you reduce your need for a cesarean.

"Yeah, I wrote a birth plan. The hospital was kind but not really interested . . . My mother was at the birth, and that was good as my husband was able to take breaks." —Hadass E.

Similarly, in anecdotes about epidurals, you must remember that they are just that: anecdotes. They likely contain little or no hard facts as might apply to your situation. "I heard . . ." should not be the foundation of any decision.

Rules and Regulations

Another aspect to consider when thinking about the birth and your birth plan are issues of legality and permissions. Different states have different laws about who can attend to a pregnant woman in labor, in what capacity, and in what situation. Homebirth, though becoming more popular, can be a tricky area. They are perfectly legal in many states; what may be tightly regulated is *who* can attend to you during a homebirth, and finding a care provider of the appropriate license status could be the challenge. Many women who have made the effort to find those legal, licensed, and compatible birth attendants have had very positive and rewarding experiences. But again, only you can decide after appropriate research if this effort is for you.

Some hospitals also have rules about nonlicensed support, nonprofessionally affiliated support, or how your support is designated. For example, many women choose to use the services of a doula, an assistant who provides nonmedical physical and emotional support during pregnancy and childbirth. Doulas can offer amazing support during the birth process, advocating for you and your partner when you are otherwise occupied and hopefully reducing complications and/or unnecessary interventions, but can't help much if they are not allowed in your room. Before you get too attached, it's worthwhile to check, double-check, and triple-check that your support team will be able to be there for you. Or maybe it's a cue to rethink where you intend to give birth.

The point is, you may have to jump through hoops to get what you think you want for your birth, and only you can decide whether the hoop jumping is the right thing to do for you. The planning for anything considered nontraditional can be quite time and energy consuming and stressful, yet it could be incredibly rewarding and empowering. It's more than the difference between the path of least resistance and another piece of work when you are already overwhelmed; it could mean the difference (and a big difference!) in how you feel about the birth experience when it is all over.

Nonbirth Aspects of the Birth Plan

One of the most effective uses of birth plans can have nothing to do with the actual birth. Your birth plan can also specify issues around the birth, such as who can visit when and so on. If you have a particularly large and/or involved family and you do or don't want them near when you give birth, your plan can state that. You get to be selfish about this!

SHEKNOWS SECRET: Hospital staff members are generally willing to help you enforce visiting "rules" dictated by your birth plan.

Some women like all their family with them at birth, and their birth plan could and should say this. In contrast, maybe you don't want everyone there; your birth plan can say this, too. And when your birth plan says it, you can put enforcement elsewhere—with your partner or even hospital staff. Believe me, the staff in labor and delivery has experience thwarting even the most determined great-aunt to-be and their priority is your health and your baby's health, not Aunt Edna's feelings.

Writing Your Birth Plan

Even though you've taken some time to think about the big picture, a birth plan can still seem overwhelming. To get a handle on all the pieces, you can begin writing down your wishes in terms of the following categories:

- General labor
- Labor induction/augmentation
- Anesthesia/pain medication
- Cesarean-section delivery
- Perineal care
- Delivery
- Afterbirth
- Newborn care
- Postpartum
- Feeding
- Visitors

To create a thorough printable birth plan or look at some of your potential options in each of these categories, visit *http://pregnancy andbaby.com/birthplan.*

Getting Buy-In

As you research and write your birth plan, it's essential to get buy-in from your partner and your medical care provider. Your medical care provider might be the easier of the two. Your medical care provider, whether a physician or midwife, has been through many births before this one and her knowledge and experience can help you develop a reasonable and realistic birth plan.

SHEKNOWS SECRET: Use your medical care provider's knowledge and experience (of other births and your particular body) to help you create your birth plan.

Don't be surprised if your partner is a little (or a lot) scared by a birth plan; supportive, yes, but scared. For some partners, pregnancy—and particularly a first pregnancy—can be a little abstract and not quite real. Even if partners gain some sympathy weight, they don't feel all the constant physical changes that you do. As a result of this, your partner may look at you blankly when you talk about birth plans initially; supportive, sure, but a bit removed from any passion or vehemence you feel on the subject.

"I'm not sure that I like the concept of a birth 'plan.' Such an overpowering, humbling, and unpredictable event can hardly be planned. But you certainly can prepare to be effective decision makers in a way that fits with the kind of birth you hope to have. Having an advocate in addition to your partner seems valuable; sometimes your partner deserves to just be a partner."
—Lauren D.

Beyond the Plan

While birth plans are a great way to think consciously about how you want the birth to go, you will not be able to control everything. Planning for birth as best as you can is one thing; getting so attached to the plan that you can't see beyond it is quite another. Contingency plans, alternate plans, being open to change—whatever you want to call it—also needs to be part of your birth plan.

It's Okay to Change Your Plan Midbirth

You can change your plans in the middle of the birth, and it's okay. Whether you come to the realization that you really do want some help from medication or don't want that epidural after all or the extra support person that you thought you'd want there is pissing you off instead, feel free to announce your new feelings. Even when you're grunting and pushing with all your might, you can bark at the nurse, "Don't say, 'Good girl!' I'm not a dog!" You can! You are the one doing all the hard work in that room.

"One of my most compelling memories was my fear of using drugs. When my first son was being born I refused any drugs, and after seven hours my mother turned to me and said, 'Honey, I'm not sure why you're afraid to utilize the resources available to you that can make you feel better, but you can either choose to enjoy the end of this experience or not.' I immediately got an epidural." —Angie T.

If the Plan Doesn't Go as Planned

Sometimes, in spite of your best effort—your research and thought and planning—a birth doesn't go as planned. When you wanted a birth without medication but ended up with an emergency cesarean section or if you really wanted the epidural but didn't get to the hospital in time or whatever situation was not what you envisioned, you may have some serious emotions to process along with regular birth hormone fluctuations. You can feel frustrated, traumatized even, and all the while grateful for the birth of your child. Processing these complex emotions can feel like grief; some around you may not understand why you are upset when you and your baby are "fine." Even if you believe it on some level, sometimes it's not so simple and easy to say, "We're healthy, so it's all okay."

Take Time to Process What Happened

Becoming a mother is, obviously, life changing, and birth is a complex emotional and physical time. A birth that doesn't go as planned can impact the first days of bonding with your baby, your longer-term recovery, and possibly a future pregnancy. You may need more time and emotional space than you expected to process all the emotions around your birth, whether it went exactly according to plan or totally haywire. You need to find some validation for your very real feelings. With luck, your partner and your care team can give that to you. Ask for it if you need to.

Thinking about Next Time

At the absolute minimum, a not-quite-as-planned birth can be a learning experience you can apply to future pregnancies and births. Maybe that's all you need. But maybe you can take that experience and turn it into a jumping-off point for a new phase of your life; how can you make absolutely sure that doesn't happen again and how can you help others? Where will that lead you? It can even lead to a new career (really!).

Every birth experience is truly different, and each is equally valid. We each must process it in our own way. Whether you had the perfect or far-from-perfect birth experience, you do have a beautiful baby and life with that baby to look forward to.

Part II
YOUR BABY

CHAPTER 5

Sleep When the Baby Sleeps, and Other Unattainable Dreams

You did it! You delivered a baby! One moment your baby was on the inside, and the next you're holding her. Can you believe it? You are no longer a mother-to-be or an expectant mother; you're a new mom or just Mom.

The first moments after birth are something to savor; you will never have them again. Take a mental snapshot, or twenty or a hundred. Etch these images in your brain, write the feelings on your soul—even if the feeling is exhaustion and bewilderment. One day, that child will ask you what it was like when she was born and you will explain that for just a fraction of a moment, time did indeed stand still as you saw her for the first time. The wonder and miracle of conception is now tangible; you are holding her.

Take It All In

This little person that you have been waiting to meet for so long is here in your arms. Does he look anything like you thought he would? Does he have hair? Doubtless, you've counted the fingers and toes several times already just to be sure they are all there. Has she already wrapped your husband around her little finger, ensuring a lifetime of serious spoiling? Does he look nothing like you expected and more like an alien?

Within moments, it's all busy again—and even if it's done quietly in the most subdued of birth experiences, it's busy—activity around you and the baby, making sure both of you are okay. Questions float through the air. "What's his name?" your doctor asks. "How much does she weigh?" the labor nurse wants to know. There are instructions, too. "Lean back," some voice calls out, "we still need to deliver the placenta." And all you want to do is see this little human you managed to grow and birth.

Next comes an odd juxtaposition: the euphoric adrenaline high of what you have just accomplished coupled with the total physical exhaustion of what you have just accomplished. I remember being suddenly wide awake and alert even though moments before I thought I would pass out from the exhaustion of labor and delivery that lasted longer than a few marathons. I was feeling so many things all at once. It was one of the happiest moments of my life, and one of the most physically confusing. I was so euphoric with love for my son, love for my husband, proud and amazed at the labor I just endured and achieved, yet physically wrecked beyond words.

Animal Magnetism?

For many women, the powerful instant love and a corresponding urge to protect their newborn can be shocking. As much as you try to prepare yourself for meeting your child face to face for the first time, this primal protective instinct can seem to arise out of nowhere. It's more than love, it's more than joy, it's something deeper. You can become hyperaware of all that is going on around your baby, almost to the point of ignoring yourself.

"After my second son was born, I was surprised that my emotions were not as intense. I felt more practical, or something, in those first hours after his birth. We were thrilled, of course, but I specifically remember that it took a few days for me to get to a deeper sort of attachment." —Lauren D.

While many women do fall in love with their babies instantly, some women don't feel that bond immediately. That can be confusing, too. It's okay to admit it if your baby does look wrinkly and weird to you, not adorable and cute. (All those "newborns" you're used to seeing on television are months old.) Given what you and your body have just been through, you may feel some detachment in those first moments. You may wonder if that baby is really yours. Did all that just happen? Or are you in some intense, profoundly realistic dream—and when will you wake up already?

SHEKNOWS SECRET: It's okay if it takes you a little while to develop a strong bond with the baby. Given the intense physical and emotional experience of birth, some confusing emotions are normal.

New Roles and Responsibilities

I remember being shocked in the first hours after our first child was born. The nurses kept asking me questions about what I wanted for our son. They knew we planned to keep him in my room and they actively supported that, but they asked if I wanted a couple hours of sleep after my long labor (promising not to feed him or anything else I didn't want). My initial thought was, "Huh?" then, "Oh, yeah, I'm the mom. I get to decide these things." Just like it took me some time to wrap my head around the idea of being pregnant eight-and-a-half months prior, it took some active thinking to wrap my head around the reality that our son was really here, separate from my body. Or maybe it was just the physical exhaustion of childbirth.

You're in Charge

You have a new authoritative role. When the nurse comes in and asks a question, you get to make the decision. If there's anything you don't like, it's also your responsibility to speak up, to grasp that authority confidently. *Of course I'll do that,* you might be thinking. In reality, it can take a mental leap to transform the visceral and emotional protectiveness you feel into appropriate decision making.

. . . But You're Second Banana

Soon enough, within minutes sometimes, the visiting and informing starts, and with that you have yet another new role—second banana. While you were pregnant, you were the star of the show; the focus was on you and on your belly. But as soon as that baby is out, people—family, friends, acquaintances, even strangers—want a piece of that baby. They want to hold her and look at her. They'll ask you the cursory questions, and even be (somewhat) interested in the answers, but what they really want is that baby. And they want to tell you just the right way to do everything for that baby, as if you don't know what you are doing.

MORE Advice

Yup, just about everyone starts to give advice and tell you what great thing worked for them and what you should never do, and whether you do or don't know what you're doing is irrelevant to them. This advice comes from the same well-intentioned and loving vat of advice as most of the comments of the pregnancy police—it's essentially a continuation of the pregnancy police. But this time you are almost secondary.

"I remember feeling really isolated and disconnected when I was first at home. My sister's friend confided it was the loneliest time of her life when she was living in a condo with her firstborn and there was no one around. Boy, did that make me feel better!"
—*Kellie B.*

Sleep when the baby sleeps—everyone tells you that. And it's great advice, except that for the first few days and weeks it seems like everyone wants to meet this new little person. And every time the baby sleeps, those everyones assume that'd be a good time to get your undivided attention so you can tell them all about the baby and the birth. You'll sleep the *next* time the baby sleeps, they may think. Apparently, sleep when the baby sleeps doesn't apply to the time they are spending with you.

Swaddle her tightly; don't swaddle her tightly. Hold his head higher; move his head that way. This is how you burp; this is how you diaper. All this advice, so well meaning, may or may not work for you. Just as your pregnancy is unique, so is this baby, and what works to feed and soothe this baby is going to take some trial and error (and the error part can be exceedingly frustrating). It may even change day to day!

> *"You know more than you think you do."*
> *—Dr. Benjamin Spock*

It's easy for the advice givers to forget this in their enthusiasm—they themselves had to go through trial and error to learn parenting when their children were tiny. So often, mostly thanks to the hormones and uncertainty of my new role, I thought the constant commentary was a statement on my mothering, even though it wasn't.

SHEKNOWS SECRET: People's advice is simply that—it's not a judgment on your parenting skills.

At some point, I realized that the people giving advice were trying to share their hard-won knowledge based on their own experiences. When they'd become parents for the first time, they had no idea what they were doing either, and they had family members and friends giving them just this same sort of advice. And they were likely as fragile as I was, though the years may have made those memories fade.

Help Versus "Help"

Your family can be a great resource for you in the early days. The enthusiasm of many grandparents, aunts, uncles, and cousins is real and palpable—and they may inadvertently overstep bounds. It's *your* baby, not your mother-in-law's, not your mother's, not your sister's or your cousin's. Yours. Remember that new authoritative role you recognized in the moments after your child's birth? It may well be time to exercise it a little.

SHEKNOWS SECRET: Ask someone to help you manage family members who overstep their bounds.

In the first hours and days after the baby is born, when everyone descends on you, you're often still experiencing a postbirth adrenaline surge. You may be tired, even exhausted, but this mothering thing is still such a new experience that you may not yet need help. It's exciting and scary, and possibly, that excitement and fear is what is keeping you going in the short term rather than appropriate rest—or as appropriate as can be managed for the situation.

"People who say they sleep like a baby usually don't have one." —Leo J. Burke

If you are lucky enough to have family that will come and help after the baby is born, it is worth the time to think about what kind of help you may need and when you will need it. Perhaps you could consider talking to family or friends about being flexible about when they come and help now. You might need more help at specific times of the day than others, or even a couple weeks after the birth than in the first days home. And see if they are as comfortable helping with the laundry as they are holding the baby.

Handling Visitors

The first few days to couple of weeks after the birth of your baby should be all about supporting you and your partner as you get to know your new family member. It's a time you need meals brought to you and someone else to deal with the cleaning. It's so obvious, but easier said than done.

> *"I was scared and overwhelmed, I told my husband 'I want our old life back. . . .' My husband's family is big and they would just start handling my three-week-old daughter and passing her around. She would get overhandled and then feel upset, and start to fuss. It freaked me out and I would make an excuse and take her upstairs." —Lynne T.*

SHEKNOWS SECRET: You get to say no to visitors!

One of the worst ways to overdo it is to let yourself be run ragged by the whims of others. Everyone wants a piece of the baby, but you can say no! It's hard, but you can. Sure, you want your cousins or dear friends to meet your baby, but when they call and ask when they can come over, you absolutely get to say when would work best for you. If one of those times doesn't work for them, you don't have to give in or change your routine to accommodate them.

The Baby Blues or Something More?

Postbirth, your body continues to go through some tremendous hormonal changes. Coupled with the general anxiety of new parenthood, and sometimes sadness in the first days after the birth of your baby, "baby blues" is quite common.

"I was young when I got pregnant—I was only 19—and I wasn't married. My parents were immensely supportive. They would have given me the clothes off their backs to keep me and the baby happy and healthy. My extended family was a little more ambivalent." —Ruth D.

While baby blues often resolves itself in a few weeks after birth without long-term effects, sometimes it is something more serious. Our society is becoming more aware of postpartum depression and longer-term impact on mothers and kids. If feelings of sadness don't resolve fairly shortly after the birth of your baby—and after you have attempted to address possible contributing factors (such as intrusive family and friends or advice that is contrary to your instinct)—contact your medical care provider for some consultation and professional support.

SHEKNOWS HOW TO IDENTIFY POSTPARTUM DEPRESSION

When it comes to postpartum depression (PPD), most moms think, "Well, that won't be me." What many women don't realize is that it really might happen to them—between one-quarter and one-half of all women experience some form of a postpartum depressive illness. You may start showing signs of baby blues three to five days after your baby is born. If you feel that way for longer than a couple weeks, it may be the sign of a bigger problem for which you need help. Just some of the signs of PPD include:

- Tired all the time
- Unable to sleep well
- Crying a lot, even about little things
- Trouble remembering things
- Trouble concentrating or confusion
- Feelings of guilt or inadequacy
- Irritability or hostility
- Anxiety
- Inability to cope
- Lack of interest in the baby
- Hyper-concerned for the baby
- Headaches or chest pains
- Uncaring about how you look
- Not wanting to leave the house

For more information on identifying and coping with PPD, check out *http://PregnancyAndBaby.com/pregnancy/ Pregnancy-Postpartum-Postpartum-Depression*. In addition, this postpartum contract tool is designed to help your partner and family help you when it might be hard for you to help yourself: *http://PregnancyAndBaby.com/downloads/ ppdpromise.pdf*.

You Will Survive!

Tired doesn't begin to describe your exhaustion; you are functionally a zombie. Welcome to early parenthood. Millions—no, billions—of parents have been through this before you. I have a piece of very good news for you: We survived and so will you, even if you don't feel like it now. And the feeling fades, even if the memory endures.

Ask any parent about those early days, and you'll likely hear something like, "You just don't know until you've gone through it" or "I can't describe it." Each of them is right; enduring those intensely sleep-deprived days of early parenting is like joining a club. You just don't know until you're in it, and even then you don't have much perspective until the day you wake up and you realize you (and the baby) just had more sleep than you've had in weeks. It's a glimmer of hope. Even though you haven't quite made it through this phase completely, you feel, just maybe, there is hope again.

Accept the Upheaval

In the first few weeks of your baby's life, he is developing and growing at a pace that is hard to fathom. From a crying, pooping lump to an emerging awareness of the world around him to actual interaction, it's a huge transition. Think daily leaps and bounds. Your child has gone from a relatively quiet, dark, watery, and warm world to this bright, loud, super-stimulating, and temperature-variable world. It takes more than a little getting used to, for both of you.

"(Yawn) Oh, did you just ask me something? I think I was so tired I just don't remember." —Debby S.

If you think about times of great transition in your adult life, you'll realize that routine got thrown out the window and you needed to figure it all out from scratch. If you start a new job or move to a new house or town, you have to figure out new routes, new standards. That's what's happening with your child, every single day. The difference is that we have tools of experience and language with which to communicate with others and ourselves about what is happening. Your new baby, though, has no idea what is happening, and has only one way to communicate: crying.

SHEKNOWS SECRET: For you, for your child, every day is going to be different for a while.

So accept that you're in a time of transition now, and today is not going to be the same as yesterday. What worked yesterday in terms of settling down and possible sleep might not work today—it might, but it might not. With so much stimuli coming in so rapidly, it's no wonder your baby can be a little bit of a mess at times—and that translates right over to you being a mess, too.

Stop Fighting So Hard

It can be so tempting to create a schedule early on. But since you can't schedule the baby's developmental bursts and peaks and valleys, and fighting against them just makes everyone even crankier, I'm going to suggest something that may sound a little crazy at first: Give in.

"If one feels the need of something grand, something infinite, something that makes one feel aware of God, one need not go far to find it. I think that I see something deeper, more infinite, more eternal than the ocean in the expression of the eyes of a little baby when it wakes in the morning and coos or laughs because it sees the sun shining on its cradle."
—Vincent van Gogh

That's right; just give in to the ups and downs. Give in to the variable sleep, the crankiness—yours and the baby's. You aren't going to get the dishes done right after eating (and you should be getting help for that anyway!), but neither are you going to just frustrate yourself by fighting so hard against everything. And when you give in, you're more likely to recognize the small beauties of the day: the colorful sunrise, the brightness of the full moon casting shadows across the lawn, the soft cooing of your baby when she finally does settle to sleep, the understanding in your dog's eyes, or just how good that hot water feels on your shoulders when you do get to shower.

SHEKNOWS SECRET: Set no or very low expectations—you'll be less likely to be disappointed. Give in to the nonschedule!

When you get frustrated with this process of learning about your baby and trying to figure out what she wants, the baby feels it. If you are stressed, you are more tense, and when you're tense you don't even hold your baby as comfortably. Think about it in adult terms: You can tell when your partner is stressed—you can *feel* it—and you respond to that. So, too, can your baby feel it when you're stressed, and she will respond accordingly.

Schedule Versus Routine

I probably haven't convinced you that not having a schedule is okay, but think of it this way: Who would that schedule really be for? You, of course. It would all be so much easier for *you* if that baby would adhere to a real schedule. You'd be able to get so much done! You'd be in control! Rarely, though, does it actually work like that. Yes, your child will derive benefit from it eventually (kids—older babies and children—do tend to thrive on routine), but in these early days and weeks, not so much.

"I don't remember the first several weeks of my son's life because I was so exhausted. I wasn't getting more than two hours of sleep a night. I didn't have anyone to help me—I was raising him alone—and it took a huge physical toll on me. That part was awful. People talk about how terrible diapers and baby puke are, but I'd take poopy diapers over sleep deprivation any day."
—Ruth D.

What about, instead of creating a rigid schedule, saying, "The baby eats at 10:00 A.M. and goes down for a nap at 10:30 A.M.," you look for general patterns toward the goal of identifying a routine? Does your baby generally follow a pattern of eat-alert time-fuss-sleep-repeat every three to four hours? Or maybe it's alert time-eat-sleep-fuss? Both of those are patterns you can work with to find some expectedness to your day, maybe plan things around (generally). They aren't schedules, per se, but they do allow for some predictability. Though you might not have an exact time, such routines help you to know that sometime mid-morning there will be a feeding and likely a nap after that. Even so, watch out for changes.

SHEKNOWS SECRET: Instead of obsessing about a schedule, look for patterns and tendencies that can help you build a daily routine.

Can You Spoil an Infant?

You might think—and you might be told—that if you don't put your baby on a schedule, you are spoiling him. I don't buy it. At this very young age, babies can't be spoiled; they can only be cared for. This is another area where others will give plenty of advice. They mean well, but just nod and say thank you and know you are going to have to figure it all out for yourself, based on your relationship with your baby. Yes, your child needs to learn to sleep on his own, do many things on his own, but does he have to learn it all in the first month?

"The priority shift is a relief. There are so many things that used to monopolize my time and my energy that I realize now, in the face of being a mother, are just completely irrelevant." —Debra Messing

What does it mean to spoil a baby? It's one of those things that members of a certain older generation love to tell us not to do.

"Don't hold the baby too much! You'll spoil him!" For spoiling to really happen, the baby—child, really—has to have reached a certain level of intellectual development. He needs the ability to engage in willful manipulation, which he can't do for a while yet. Sure, babies are self-centered, but they really don't have the capacity to understand the world around them in full. They feel discomfort, hunger, overstimulation, and can only think about themselves, but expecting empathy from a newborn is about four or five years too soon. Given all that, do you really think your tiny baby is capable of being spoiled? True, there will be a time your child needs to learn some lessons about waiting and responding appropriately to situations and so on, but is it really now?

SHEKNOWS SECRET: At this point in your baby's life, he doesn't have the intellectual capacity to be spoiled. He simply wants his needs met.

Babies, in their total vulnerability, depend on us to respond to their needs. Yes, they need to learn to fall asleep, and if you've met all their needs (fed, burped, freshly diapered, appropriately warm, and so on), letting them fuss a bit isn't the worst thing in the world, but this is a trust-building exercise. Your baby is learning to trust that you will meet his needs, and you'll be able to trust that when your baby fusses something needs to be addressed. It's a give and take, really, but with only one side understanding the bigger picture.

"When my second child was born, I had a vision of me and my baby blissfully spending time together in a spotlessly clean house. I spent a significant amount of time trying to keep things clean. Now cleanliness does make me feel peaceful and happy, but I do wish I had decided to put everything on hold for a few months and focus only on my baby." —Jen O.

Missing Your Old Life

Your old life probably looks appealing about now: Uninterrupted sleep; your time was your own; you could jet off to Paris on a moment's notice if you wanted to—even if you never did. You may feel guilty for thinking about it, for missing it, but you are not the first and definitely won't be the last to miss your old life. Babies are hard sometimes!

SHEKNOWS SECRET: Allow yourself to miss your old life. It doesn't make you selfish or petty.

Grieving your old life may seem like a selfish, silly thing to do—especially when you had many months to prepare for this time, and possibly planned on being a parent for a very long time—but it is a natural part of transitioning. Allowing yourself a little space in your head to recognize that you'll miss certain things, maybe didn't appreciate them as much as you thought you did, can help you move forward and accept this new very bleary phase of your life.

"Tired is the new black." —Amy Poehler

This Won't Last Forever

How long is this deeply bleary time going to last? That all depends on your baby. Every baby is different. Some babies sleep for longer stretches earlier; some take much longer. Some find a routine earlier than others. You just never know until you are in it.

"It is a seemingly endless blur, but it truly passes quickly, and before you know it you can actually finish sentences again or remember where you set something down!" —Kellie B.

In the end, though, it's a very short period of time in your and your baby's life. One day, it will be a little different. One day, there'll be more interaction. One day, there'll be a smile. One day, it will somehow, without you realizing it or making any specific efforts, be easier.

No matter what path you choose, whether no schedule, very scheduled, or something in between, you are going to have a moment that makes all of it worthwhile and makes going forward that much easier. Maybe it's the first truly interactive smile from your child that melts it all away or a stretch of sleep or a day when your low expectations were met, and then some. Whatever it is, this hard time is very much worth it.

CHAPTER 6

Your Body, Rearranged

By the end of your pregnancy, you're tired of the aches, the inability to move the way you used to, the swelling, the fatigue. You not only want to be able to see your toes again, you want to be able to bend over and touch them. As much as you have enjoyed being pregnant (or not), and as happy as you are about having a baby, you want your body back, and now that the baby is here, your body is yours again! Right? Not so fast. It doesn't quite work that way.

The Healing Process

Your body needs to undergo a lot of recovery postbirth, and it's not going to happen overnight. It's likely going to take longer than you think it is and, honestly, your body will never be quite the same again. And just as body-image issues don't develop overnight, they don't immediately disappear with the delivery of your baby, either. You won't be wearing your prepregnancy wardrobe just yet— definitely keep those skinny jeans in the back of the closet for a little while longer.

SHEKNOWS SECRET: Just because the baby has been born doesn't mean that your body is yours again.

Immediately after the birth of your baby, whether you delivered vaginally or by cesarean section, your body is battered. Stretched, squeezed, pulled, poked, and battered. Either you've pushed all the muscles, ligaments, and other tissues in your nether regions to their limits or you've had major abdominal surgery. You may have some deep soreness and bruising. You have to have some respect for this; even if you feel pretty good immediately after the birth, your body has some repair work to do. No, a lot of repair work to do.

The Persistent Belly — and More

I remember being stunned by how pregnant I still looked in the first days after our son was born. Intellectually, I knew I wouldn't be back to my old self anytime soon, but it was shocking—I still looked pregnant. Even though I knew it was going to take time for the extra fluids to pass, for the skin and tissues to shrink back, it was still disconcerting. My maternity clothes still fit just fine; there were no "regular" clothes in sight for me.

"The thing that surprised me the most about my post-birth body is how nonelastic my skin apparently is. I have friends who blew up as big as a house during pregnancy and didn't get a single stretch mark. I lost the weight quickly, but my stomach looks like a war zone. A flabby one." —Ruth D.

Too Much Is Too Much

Your doctor or other medical care provider will likely recommended an activity level for the first days and weeks after the birth. If you have stitches of any kind, you will need to take care not to overstrain in whichever direction, and there are signs of potential infection of which to be aware (not fun to think about, but necessary).

SHEKNOWS SECRET: When the doctor says, "Don't overdo it!" during the first weeks after the delivery, she means it! She *is* talking to *you!*

What not overdoing it means is really listening to your body and respecting the work it has just done. Don't try to do everything—you can't, anyway. Your job in the first days and weeks after your baby is born is to care for and get to know that baby and take care of your own body. Someone else can vacuum; this is the time to ask for help, and if you are not good at asking for help, learn to be good at it. If a family member wants to come help, that person does the dishes and the laundry, not you. Friends and family who come by to see the baby can be put to work! Your body needs to rest. Period.

"I feel sexier after having a baby. I think you feel a lot more confident and much more appreciative of your body and what it's capable of doing. I've got a lot more respect for it." —Rachel Weisz

In spite of such admonitions from your medical care provider, your partner, your mother, and anyone else, there will be a day shortly after the birth of your baby when you will overdo it. You'll think, "If I don't do this, who will? And it has to be done." Even if it doesn't really *have* to be done, you'll do it—and overdo it. And you'll pay.

Some Things Get Bigger

Beyond recovery from delivery, there are other changes happening in your body. While most of you is still big even after delivery but likely on its way back to something approaching normal at some point in the not-too-distant future, there's a part of you that is going to get even bigger: your breasts. And if you are breastfeeding, they're going to stay that way for a while.

"It surprised me that it took three months to feel myself again energy-wise after both my C-sections. After my vaginal delivery, I could have gone dancing that night. The other big surprise was having to wear a G-cup bra; that was depressing especially since I am only 5'2"." —Karen W.

If you have an ample chest to begin with this may be an annoyance, but you probably already know how to deal with the girls. If you are naturally on the smaller side, however, the nursing boobs can be a shock. You'll go from a bit fuller than usual during pregnancy to oh-my-goodness-where-the-heck-did-these-come-from in several hours when your milk comes in. You may have cleavage for the very first time in your life!

SHEKNOWS SECRET: Milk production brings new meaning to the term "full figured." Emphasis on "full."

If ever there was a time to spend money on a good bra, it is now. A good nursing bra can make breastfeeding more comfortable while supporting this particular body area. You need appropriate support through some serious changes that are going to be taking place in those breasts on a daily, almost hourly, basis. Nursing bras also have hooks and snaps in the front for easier access for the baby. As you establish breastfeeding between you and your baby, the relative fullness and feel of your larger breasts will change as the baby nurses and empties one side or the other. You need appropriate support (literally) for that, and your regular bras from that well-known mall chain store aren't it.

Another Diet?

Meanwhile, as you seem to be gaining and losing ounces and pounds daily in your chest, you might start to think about losing that baby weight as quickly as possible. Go ahead, think about it. That may be as far as you get in the short term. And that's okay.

"Don't you love how celebrities claim that breastfeeding alone has been responsible for shedding all their baby weight? I had to retrain my way of thinking and eating after baby was born. I think it helps to not see it as dieting, but as being healthy for yourself and your baby—and that includes the occasional splurge! My husband actually said he liked my 'curvier' body after baby!" —Kim G.

Losing the weight you gained during pregnancy is going to take some time. More time than you think, probably. Most of us know of someone who took all the weight off almost immediately, but that's not most of us. And at this early stage, weight loss really should be secondary to taking care of the baby, letting your body recover, and eating healthy food to support those endeavors.

SHEKNOWS SECRET: For most women, it takes months and months to lose the baby weight.

Whatever you do, try to avoid reading or even glancing at the articles in the magazines about how this or that supermodel put on sixty pounds during a pregnancy and took it all off in less than six weeks. I've said it before and I will say it again: this is not normal. As with the advertised pregnancy weight gain in these women, there are extenuating circumstances. Their body types are not like yours and their lives are not like yours. Take their stories, if you must read them at all, for what they are: anomalies. Great for them but not at all great for the morale of the average new mom.

"I'm not sure if the ambivalence I felt was postbirth or post-thirty." —Lauren D.

At the same time you are thinking about eating fewer calories, you also need to be sure you are eating to support your activity calorically—and that you are adequately supporting your milk supply if you are breastfeeding. Yes, it can seem a contradiction. Crash diets are never a good idea in the first place, but they can be plain disastrous when you are postpartum. You need appropriate fuel to deal with the demands being placed on you—the key word being "appropriate." Just because you are no longer grow-ing a baby on the inside doesn't mean you should stop thinking about healthy eating. You're still growing a baby—just on the outside.

SHEKNOWS SECRET: The plain truth is that phys-ical recovery from childbirth is an extended effort.

Building a Healthy Exercise Routine

When is it time to start exercising again, or just plain start exercis-ing? If you were very active throughout your pregnancy, you may be able to start formal exercise shortly after birth. Check with your doctor before starting anything, and, again, take care not to overdo it. Your doctor can help you determine appropriate levels of exercise—both cardiovascular exercise and resistance exercise—for your fit-ness level and postpartum stage.

"At one of my postpartum checkups, my OB/GYN gave me the name and number of a plastic surgeon who could 'take care of those' stretch marks. I was not amused (and did not call the surgeon)." —Jen O.

Even if you are one of those lucky enough to get back to your prepregnancy size and weight pretty quickly, after a baby your body is never quite the same. Numbers on tape measures can be the same, but you're reproportioned. There's something that's just . . . different . . . not quite the same. Your favorite jeans may fit again, but likely never in quite the same way, and there's this softness to your lower belly that no amount of abdominal crunches quite firms up.

SHEKNOWS SECRET: After a birth, your body is different, even if you go back to the same weight and clothing size.

Rearranged . . . In a Good Way?

Body images, both prebirth and postbirth, pop up when you least expect them. You might think it will be different for you—you'll lose the weight and look the same in weeks, or be more accepting of the changes sooner. Maybe it will be different for you, but probably not. Even if you're going along, day by day, thinking you've got it under control—boom—something surprises you. You catch yourself out of the corner of your eye in the mirror and don't recognize yourself or it's weeks after the baby's birth and you're still feeling fleshy. Every woman goes through at least some of this after the birth of a baby, even the supermodels. The postpregnancy body is not the same as it was before, and it never will be.

When the mirror isn't lying to you—and oh, how you wish it would—I hope you'll remember that there's a very good reason for the changes in your body: that sweet baby. The stretch marks, the nursing boobs, the butt bigger than you imagined it could be, it was all part of growing and nurturing a new human. And that's pretty awesome.

CHAPTER 7

It's Okay to Love Your Pediatrician (and Why You Should)

After months of a fairly close relationship with your obstetrician or midwife, suddenly it's over. After monthly, biweekly, then weekly—or even more frequent—visits, you'll see that person in a few weeks for a follow-up, then it's back to the status quo yearly checkup. It can be kind of a shock, actually, particularly if you had a warm relationship with your doctor or midwife. You may even feel sad! Luckily, you have an outlet for your grief. Where do you direct all that caregiver-patient energy and affection? Yup, the baby's pediatrician.

The Pediatrician-Parent Relationship

You are going to be spending a whole lot of time with this person, even more than you spent with your obstetrician or midwife, and for a heck of a lot longer. This is the beginning of a multiyear, maybe even multidecade (if you have additional children), relationship. It's worth it to spend some time to make sure you and the pediatrician can be partners in your child's health for those many years to come. You really want to like this person. You *should* like this person. A lot.

SHEKNOWS SECRET: Spend some time choosing a pediatrician who can be your partner in your child's health for many years to come.

You'll no doubt do some research when looking for a pediatrician. But beyond credentials, proximity, insurance, and recommendations, you also have to be able to talk to this person, to communicate. The pediatrician may have impeccable credentials and a stellar reputation, but if you can't communicate with one another, it's going to be a challenging relationship. You have to be able to trust your child's pediatrician to give your child the best possible care, to look out for your child, and to talk with you openly and honestly about issues related to your child's health and well-being. Your child's pediatrician must be able to trust you to listen, consider, and do the best for your child. It's a partnership.

> *"Never go to a doctor whose office plants have died." —Erma Bombeck*

The relationship with your child's doctor is a funny thing. Pediatricians usually consider the whole family dynamic—and may be concerned about the whole family—when caring for and treating your child, but unless you see a family practice physician that actually treats the whole family, your child's doctor is not your doctor; he your child's doctor, and your child is his primary priority. You may call him "my" pediatrician, but he is not your pediatrician. The line can feel a little fuzzy at times, but remembering that distinction is important. Your child's health and well-being is the pediatrician's priority and you are both partners in that. For example, if your child needs a particular type of treatment, the pediatrician will try to find a solution that will be convenient for you as the parent in terms of frequency and/or duration or other details, but the pediatrician's bigger concern is going to be getting your child that treatment, your convenience second.

Finding a Pediatrician

Just as you did when you found your pregnancy healthcare provider, you should consider all your options when finding a doctor for your baby. Do your homework—ask for recommendations from friends or neighbors, and try to meet with a handful of "finalists."

Pediatrician Versus Family Practice

While a pediatrician is a physician who specializes in children and adolescents, family practice physicians treat adults as well as children (and they are differentiated from internists or general practitioners, who treat adults); they can treat the whole family. Whether you choose a pediatric office or a family practice office for your child's regular care depends primarily on individual preference. A pediatrician's office may be more child-centric in terms of décor, procedures, and interactions, but you may find a great family practice physician with a terrific manner with kids. And if you go with a family practice physician, your child might have her doctor for life.

Visit the Practice

While you might do fine booking a pediatrician without meeting her or visiting the practice, if the chance arises to talk with a potential physician for your child, grab it. Such meetings are an excellent opportunity to ask questions about how the practice is structured, who you might see in addition to the doctor, what happens when you need to call during off hours, and many other questions. It's also an occasion to ask yourself, "Can I work with this person? Do I feel comfortable talking to her and asking questions? Am I being rushed through this discussion?" Only you can answer those questions, and those questions are one of several factors that will help determine if this pediatrician and this pediatric practice is right for you.

> *"Our pediatrician is a calm, gentle presence. He doesn't stress you out about 'developmental milestones' and he is always telling us about his own children and grandchildren who didn't talk until age three or potty train until four. A few years ago we moved twenty miles away, but decided to stay with our pediatrician . . . a pediatrician you feel comfortable with is **that** important." —Mary Lou B.*

If the pediatrician is part of a group, you will likely see all members of that group at some time or another. One day, one doctor may see all the sick visits while the others tend to yearly physicals and other appointments. Some practices employ nurse practitioners or physician assistants who see patients for specific types of complaints. The front desk staff also has an important role in keeping the office running smoothly, and you'll see them as often as you see the doctor. Heck, depending on the popularity of the practice, you might even have more face time with the clerks than the medical staff! You may not find a practice where you really like *everybody* who works there, but a good relationship with your child's primary physician easily offsets the occasional encounter with the one grumpy older physician in the practice or the one gum-popping snarky clerk.

SHEKNOWS HOW TO FIND A DOCTOR FOR YOUR BABY
From the very first appointment or interview with a pediatrician, you should be able to tell a lot about his style of caregiving. Does he make you feel rushed or does he sit down and give you a chance to discuss things? Does he seem impatient when you ask what is probably a common question? Does he seem to be well informed and up to date on the latest pediatric medical research? If you have a specific issue or disability that affects your family, does he have a good understanding of the subject? Get more tips on our blog at *http://PregnancyAndBaby.com/blog/baby-health/*.

Consider a Pediatrician with Certain Expertise

Some pediatricians, in addition to being very good generalists for a wide range of patients, develop specific interests and a level of expertise in a specific area. This does not mean they are a board-certified expert in those areas or have the same training as a specialist, but it can mean that she can offer a little more experience in one area or another. If your family has a history of asthma or allergies, finding a pediatrician that has an interest in and works with a larger population of asthma patients might be worth the extra effort. Contact a potential practice to ask about any special interests their doctors might have.

Questions—Asking and Answering

In the first months of your child's life, you will be spending a fair bit of time in the pediatrician's office, and hopefully they will be well-baby checks only. These visits will include questions, lots of questions, from the pediatrician to you and to the pediatrician from you. You and the pediatrician are still getting to know each other, and you are both still getting to know this baby.

"We knew we'd found the perfect pediatrician for us when we guiltily asked him, at our son's two-year appointment, whether we should be worried that he still used a pacifier when he slept. Our doc responded that he 'usually only worries when the child turns five and still has a pacifier.' I think my husband and I both fell in love at that moment . . . It was so affirming to us to know we'd be supported in our parenting choices."
—Katherine A.

Answering the Doctor's Questions

Since your child's health and safety is your pediatrician's priority, he is going to be looking at you to see and sense that you are doing right by your child. Some questions he asks may seem a little odd, but there is valid reasoning behind it. You can, after answering, ask why the doctor asked a certain question. What is he trying to discern? If you can ask questions about questions without becoming defensive in the process, you may well learn something new about your child's development or a safety issue. My son's first pediatrician asked me a question about whether we had just window screens or another barrier at window level; I didn't quite understand why. So I asked, and he explained how babies and toddlers can push through even seemingly secure window screens. From what I initially thought of as a "Duh!" question, I came away with some very important safety information.

Asking Your Own Questions

When you have questions to ask the pediatrician, she should treat them with respect and understanding. Just because she has seen thousands of babies and thousands of new moms and is quite sure that this or that is going to be fine, you haven't; you're new at this. You need information and reassurance that your baby is okay and that you made the right decision choosing this medical practice.

SHEKNOWS SECRET: The pediatrician should never make you feel dumb for asking questions.

Community Respect

If you choose a local pediatrician for your child, he may also be a part of your greater civic community, and a doctor who is a part of your community is more likely to understand the very local issues affecting your child and family. That also comes with some responsibility and respect on everyone's part. If you see your child's pediatrician in the mall, it is most definitely not the time to approach him to ask about the rash on your child's arm.

Be Honest

If you want your child's pediatrician to be honest with you, you have to be honest with the pediatrician. Say what you mean and ask direct questions that will get to the information you want.

Dancing around an issue or lying wastes both of your time. If the doctor has concerns about cosleeping, for example, she may ask where the baby sleeps. If you're cosleeping and sense her concerns, you may be tempted to lie and say the baby sleeps in her crib. But know that you probably are not the first mom to come into her office that cosleeps. Trying to pretend you don't cosleep (or whatever the issue) when you do may only serve to lower the trust level if or when it becomes apparent there was some twisting or hiding of facts. Being honest is the best thing for your relationship with the pediatrician and for your baby's health.

Research Versus Anecdotes Redux

The Internet is a great tool for research on so many levels, but as with pregnancy and childbirth information, it needs to be taken in context: Whatever you read on the Internet needs to be backed up. You need facts and data; anecdotes are not valid bases for decisions for you or your child. Your brother-in-law's sister-in-law's niece's bad experience with a specific antibiotic does not mean that your child should never have it; there may be circumstances you know nothing about. Similarly, even information from a well-researched, vetted medical site doesn't mean a specific antibiotic or treatment is or is not right for your child. That's a decision to be made in partnership with the pediatrician who understands all the nuances of your child's particular situation.

Potentially Sticky Situations with the Pediatrician

If you read something on the Internet that pertains to your child's health, how you approach your pediatrician for further understanding and clarification of the issue makes a difference. Just blurting out, "I read on the Internet that . . . " may feel to a pediatrician like you are challenging years of education, training, and experience with hearsay. Instead, approach the doctor with, "I have some concerns about an issue I've read about. Can you tell me more or point me to some accurate information?" From there, you can tell him what you read online and specifically ask about the relevance of the information and validity of the source.

As an example, the issue of vaccines is a particularly challenging topic to try to sort out using valid research versus anecdote; there is so much out there that is contradictory that it almost takes specialized education to sort it out! Many pediatricians are well aware of points on both sides of the vaccination issue and willing to talk about it and provide resources. But again, approaching the topic with the pediatrician with not just the information you have gathered but also openness to a real dialog can help you understand what you found on the Internet with greater clarity and come to the best decision for your child.

If, after such discussions with your child's pediatrician, you still have issues or concerns, asking for a second opinion is reasonable. Most physicians are comfortable with this. The pediatrician may even be willing to help you find that second opinion.

The First Illness and Beyond

A significant milestone in your relationship with your child's doctor is your child's first illness. When you call—whether during office hours or off hours—the pediatrician and the practice should never make you feel like you shouldn't have called. The response should be reassuring and prompt, directing you to how much of an over-the-counter medication to give, getting you and your child in to see a medical professional as soon as possible if appropriate, or even reassuring you that, yes, you should go to the emergency room.

> *"My family practice physician was a rock star. She was still in her residency at the time, and very young— my baby was one of the first she delivered—but she treated me with absolute professionalism and respect. She was warm and kind, too, and took a genuine interest in every part of my life with my son." —Ruth D.*

As your child gets older and you are more confident in handling her illnesses, the pediatrician will also be more confident in your handling of illnesses, and you will both trust your mother's intuition if you feel something is not right. At some point, the partnership will be strong enough that you can say to your child's doctor, "There's something more going on here" and he will know what you mean, and help you take that next step immediately, whether it's an urgent visit to the hospital or a referral to a specialist.

Perfectly Imperfect

This is not to say that pediatricians are perfect—they aren't. The partnership relationship between doctor, patient, and in this case patient's parent, is critical to refining that hybrid of science, skill, and care as it applies to your child. A good relationship can and should go beyond growth statistics, well-child visits, ear infections, and vaccines to be a reference and guide to developmental ages and stages that are to come.

SHEKNOWS SECRET: Medicine is an art, not an exact science, and doctors are human.

Treating your child's pediatrician as a partner—really communicating and working with her—is also essential to modeling appropriate care provider-patient relationships for your child going forward.

CHAPTER 8

Feeding Your Baby: Milk to Macaroni and Cheese to . . . Mangoes?

As if anxiety over diet and weight gain while pregnant (and subsequent loss of that weight after the birth) isn't enough, now you get to obsess about how your baby is eating. Is she getting enough to eat? Is she gaining weight? Enough weight? Too much? From the moment your baby is born until—well, forever—you are going to be concerned with her nutrition. I bet your mom is still probably concerned about what you eat. The stereotype of the mother encouraging her adult child to eat exists for a reason.

The Breast-Bottle Divide

The breast-versus-bottle debate is probably the earliest issue over feeding your child you will encounter. It's a doozy, too.

Moms tend to feel strongly about the subject of breast versus bottle. They either want to breastfeed or they definitely do not. Beyond personal feelings, more and more research demonstrates the superiority of breastfeeding in terms of nutrition for the baby, bonding of mother and baby, even helping the new mom lose some of that pregnancy weight. The American Academy of Pediatrics recommends "exclusive breastfeeding for the first 6 months of life." Great strides have been made in the last couple of decades toward increasing the percentage of mothers in the United States who breastfeed their babies exclusively, and the length of time for which they do so. After many prior decades of declines in breast-feeding, this is a good thing.

Breastfeeding Is Easy . . . Right?

It sounds so simple—though admittedly weird to some people—and in many situations it *is* so simple: The baby latches on to the mother's breast for a perfect meal. No mixing, no warming, no bottles to clean, totally portable and easily available; it's the ultimate fast food, but far healthier for the baby than the drive-thru is for you. Mammary glands are part of what define us as mammals!

"My opinion is that anybody offended by breastfeeding is staring too hard." —David Allen

I'm not going to hide this: I breastfed. Thing is, I really didn't think I'd be into it. Before my first son was born and through the first couple of weeks of getting our breastfeeding relationship established, I thought I'd breastfeed my son for six to nine months because it was the healthiest thing to do for him, then we'd switch to formula. I worried, among other things, that it would feel some-how sexual (it never did) or that I wouldn't be able to produce enough milk to support my baby (turns out it's usually a fairly simple economic formula of supply and demand). I never dreamed that it would be such a wonderful experience for me. I never did make that formula switch.

Not Always!

The truth is that getting breastfeeding established can be a tricky thing. For some women, it's as easy as popping that baby on the breast and, voila! But for others, it can take quite a while to get in sync, and in some cases it may never work out. Even some women who establish and are committed to breastfeeding encounter difficulties at some point. For example, early on my nipples got a little sore—no, a lot sore—and every latch was a "YOWZA! THAT HURTS!" moment of tensing my body and visibly wincing before all was right again. But sticking it out a few days was all it took and my son and I never had an issue again. Later, I dealt with mastitis (an infection of a milk duct) and experienced concerns with my milk supply.

Breastfeeding as Empowerment . . .

Just as some women feel empowered by giving birth, some moms feel empowered by breastfeeding their babies.

. . . In a Good Way

Being able to feed my children with milk I made for them was kind of an astonishing experience. In our bust-glorifying society, my, um, smaller-than-average chest was kind of an issue for me. With breastfeeding, I evened the playing field in some way. Yeah, they're small (when not breastfeeding big), but look what they can do! They can grow babies! By six months old, my son was more than 20 pounds—all on milk I made for him. It was an ego boost, to be sure. At a time when I was feeling unsure about my parenting skills in other areas, it was a success I could hold on to.

"I did feel pressure to breastfeed. I am glad I did, and I do feel like it was important both from the standpoint of nutrition and as a bonding experience. However, some people take breastfeeding to a manic level. I never understood how one mother could be so harshly critical of another over something like breastfeeding."
—Jen O.

Some people don't understand breastfeeding, why you would want to use your breasts in that way. And some of those comments can come from where you least expect it. Many of our mothers were not a part of the breastfeeding era. Their misunderstanding of the benefits you are trying to impart to your child by breastfeeding may add further stress to your situation and your decision. But it is your decision.

. . . And in a Less-Than-Helpful Way

Breastfeeding women, especially avid ones, can be a smug and judgmental lot. They believe they are giving their children a superior food, and often don't understand why other mothers wouldn't do the same. Some mothers look down their noses at formula-feeding moms, question them (hopefully silently), or don't believe them when they say they had problems and couldn't breastfeed. If formula-feeding moms admit they flat out didn't want to breastfeed, breastfeeding moms judge even more.

SHEKNOWS SECRET: If breastfeeding works for you, great. But don't make formula-feeding moms feel bad about their decision. Every mom has to make her own choices.

In addition to being totally unkind and counterproductive, that attitude prevents breastfeeding moms from hearing and understanding when women do have real problems with breastfeeding or have personal issues that make using their breasts in this manner difficult. It's one of the ways women can be cruelest to one another. While some breastfeeding moms truly want nonbreastfeeding moms to understand and enjoy the experience as they have, it just doesn't always work that way. For some women, breastfeeding is not a pleasant experience. Each side of the debate needs to respect other moms' decisions to do what is best for them.

When Breastfeeding Doesn't Work

Some women have real challenges trying to breastfeed. From anatomy issues such as inverted nipples and breast-reduction surgery to health issues—the baby's or the mom's—sometimes breastfeeding is not so simple or just not possible. And when women who have these challenges try their hardest to breastfeed but ultimately aren't successful, it can feel like a major failure, emotionally and physically. We fellow moms shouldn't be looking down on them, pitying their formula-fed baby; we should be supporting them. Because in the end, they didn't fail if they kept their baby healthy and thriving, whether by breast or formula. In so many such situations, we are fortunate that safe formula-feeding is an option.

Working with a Lactation Consultant

Though breastfeeding my sons was relatively easy, my daughter and I had a different experience. We went through several weeks of trying to get our nursing relationship established, and it was excruciatingly painful on an emotional level for me as we kept not-quite getting there. I was at my wit's end. I thought hard about grabbing some formula.

"Our twins were born at thirty-seven weeks. I committed myself to breastfeeding early on in my pregnancy, but like so many challenges to come, I had no idea what I would be getting myself into! It took significant work to get nursing established, but both kids remained enthusiastic nursers until they were about two. I look back on those nursing years very fondly. The early weeks may have been punctuated by worry and frustration, but ultimately it was one of the most rewarding periods of my life."
—Victoria P.

I was extremely fortunate to find a great lactation consultant nearby who came to my house to help me problem solve. My insurance covered some of the cost (again, I was extremely lucky), and my daughter and I were able to continue our nursing relationship. Although it was never the easy process it was with my sons—I constantly had to watch my milk supply—for me, it was worth the effort.

SHEKNOWS SECRET: Visit the International Lactation Consultant Association *(www.ilca.org)* or La Leche League International *(www.llli .org)* to find a lactation consultant in your area.

Even after the breastfeeding relationship is established, you can encounter further challenges with growth spurts, figuring out pumping at work, your baby responding to your diet, or the comments of others. There's always something to obsess about. A good relationship with a kind and competent lactation consultant can be extremely helpful; most pediatricians are not breastfeeding experts.

Choosing the Bottle

With so many factors in each of our lives, only you can make the decision whether formula-feeding or breastfeeding is right for you, your baby, and your family. Consider what is right for your baby's health and your emotional and physical health. You may have some issue that makes breastfeeding extremely difficult for you, emotionally or physically, and you shouldn't be made to feel inferior for that.

> *"My breastfeeding experience was very satisfying. I didn't always love it, I didn't always savor 'the moment,' and in the middle of the night, I could feel downright resentful. I didn't follow a pristine nursing diet. I was graced with the ability to nourish and nurture my boys in this way, and it was fulfilling to have this link with them—a link that bonded us and that fueled their growth and development."*
> *—Lauren D.*

Friends and strangers who had wonderful experiences with breastfeeding may make comments about your decision to formula-feed. They may not understand why you would make such a choice, but it's not any of their business. Their comments may add to your stress, but be confident in your decision; you know your baby and your situation best. The ultimate success of a feeding plan is a healthy and thriving child and happy mama. If anyone has the audacity to challenge your decision, a simple, "I'm the mom and I am doing what I think is best for my situation," should shut them right up.

SHEKNOWS SECRET: Antiformula-feeding comments may add to your stress, but be confident in your decision. You know your baby and your situation best.

Visiting online mom-to-mom forums such as the ones at *www.sheknows.com* can help you connect with other women who've made the decision to formula-feed.

When Do We Use That High Chair?

Just when you have the breastfeeding or bottle-feeding thing down, it's time to start talking solids. Like the bottle-versus-breast battle, it seems everyone has an opinion on solids—when, what, why, how. And now that you will be varying your child's diet beyond breast-milk or formula, you start to worry about the balance of nutrients going into your child's belly.

"Ask your child what he wants for dinner only if he's buying."
—Fran Lebowitz

Some mothers and grandmothers will tell you to start putting cereal in a baby's bottle fairly early on, at weeks old even. They mean well—they think they are going to help you get more sleep—but that's not necessarily the case. It might work for some babies, but sleep length has more to do with other developmental milestones than with how much they've eaten.

When to start solids in any form is a discussion for you and your baby's pediatrician. Some go for earlier (around four months) and some later (around six months), and some still later. The pediatrician can help you determine the right developmental stage to begin solids with your baby.

SHEKNOWS SECRET: Your child (and her pediatrician) will tell you when she is ready to try some solid food.

Your child will also tell you when she is ready to try something new. My first son, just shy of six months old, sitting in my lap while I ate some yogurt one day, grabbed my hand and tried to guide the spoon to his mouth. He'd been staring at me intently for weeks as I ate food. I took it all as signs that he was ready for solid food.

First Foods Fun

When foods are introduced to babies, it's less about nutrition initially than it is about a texture and taste experience, and about testing for allergens. The baby is still getting all the nutrition he needs from your breastmilk or from formula. This, I hope, is a sign that early food introductions can be fun for all of you. Really, they can! More obsessing when your son won't eat any protein can come later (and it will come).

"I feed my kids everything, whether I think they will like it or not. And I don't make a special meal for my kids (I do not run a restaurant). If they see you eating and enjoying food, they will be more inclined to try the same food."
—Debby S.

Cereal

Cereal is often the first food given to babies, with rice or oat high on the list because they are the least allergenic. I can't think of anything more boring than thick breastmilk-tasting cereal. But then again, I'm not a baby. Some babies love this stage, rolling the new texture of food around on their tongues and in their mouths. Some look at you as if to say, "What was the point of that? I wanted what you're having!" Just make sure your child isn't showing signs of sensitivity toward the cereals, as this could indicate bigger food allergen issues.

Making Your Own Baby Food

While your baby is plotting to get your food, you may be thinking, "I'm supposed to get excited about feeding my baby those dull colored jars of puréed everything?" Well, not exactly. Home-made baby food, on the other hand, can be lots of fun because it's exceedingly simple to make yourself and you don't have to be a certain home-style guru to do it.

SHEKNOWS SECRET: Baby food can be lots of fun to make because it's simple and inexpensive to do.

Some commercial baby-food producers have gotten the clue that gray chicken paste or artificially colored anything with lots of fillers is not going to cut it anymore. In recent years, many local and/or organic sources of packaged baby food for every stage from smooth to chunky to finger food have appeared in grocery stores. But they can be pretty pricey, even budget breakers. Knowing how to whip up a few things yourself is more than a little handy. There are several very good books available that discuss preparing baby food (think steamer, food processor, and ice cube trays) in detail, and most have food introduction charts and guidelines for offering new foods and observing for likes, dislikes, allergies, and so on. Seeking out a resource with a tone and approach you like is worth the effort; ask the moms around you for their favorites.

Stick with It

Your baby might not like a new food or texture the first time you offer it, but might love it the second time and then be so over it the fourth time. Sometimes they may just not feel like eating. Again, at this introduction stage, it's all just fun and games and the nutritional worry should (and will!) come later. Feeding time can be about more than just eating. Those little peas and soft carrots are great for developing fine motor skills and finger dexterity.

SHEKNOWS SECRET: Your child gets a bib (hopefully a large one), but you should consider putting on an old t-shirt over your clothes

when you feed your child—especially if it's a
morning before work and you'd rather not have
your colleagues spy applesauce drying on your
jacket lapel.

The Transitioning Diet

As your baby gets closer to the one-year mark, breastfeeding or
formula-feeding will decline as she gets more and more nutrition
from solid foods. This is when more worrying tends to begin. You'll
likely wonder if your child is getting enough protein, vegetables,
grains, fruits, and so on. It's completely normal to worry, but just
as your meals as an adult aren't always perfect every day, worrying
about every meal being a perfect balance every day for your baby
is just going to wear you down.

SHEKNOWS SECRET: Looking at your child's diet
over the span of a few days helps you see the
slightly bigger nutritional picture.

If you think about the balance of nutrients your child is getting
over a couple or several days, as long as you are providing a range
of food to create a balance you'll have a better picture of whether
she is, on the whole, getting everything. Maybe one day she eats a
whole bunch of scrambled eggs but doesn't want egg or any other
protein the next day, but then the day after that eats tofu cubes.
Looking at the slightly bigger picture can give you a better sense
of your child's diet on the whole and whether there might be a
problem, or no problem at all.

SHEKNOWS SECRET: A single imperfect meal (or even a few) isn't going to sabotage your child's long-term eating habits.

If your child's diet becomes really limited after an initial few months of fun and diverse eating, call the pediatrician. Thanks to their experience, they probably have some good tips and tricks to offer.

The "Eww" Stage

What kids love as babies and small children sometimes doesn't continue into toddlerhood or beyond. Your one-year-old may love spinach and mushroom quesadillas, but a year later won't touch them. More than one mother has lamented the sudden addition of the word "Eww" to a child's vocabulary, with associated facial expression.

When the "Eww" stage hits, should you just pare down to just what your child will eat? I didn't, but some moms do. While I find it painful to waste food, I also find it painful to give my child the same meal day after day after day. Variations, even small ones, were necessary to my sanity as my kids entered this phase. Eventually—and it was a long eventually—my kids moved out of the "Eww" stage. Slowly, slowly they started eating more foods. So keep offering a variety of healthy foods.

SHEKNOWS SECRET: Keep offering healthy foods even if your child refuses them now. It may take a decade, but they will come around.

CHAPTER 9

Sleep: The Elephant in the Room (and It Isn't Stuffed)

Sleep is a looming topic, sometimes discussed *ad nauseam* and sometimes ignored in hopes the issue will go away. It's something underappreciated and usually underutilized in adults, and it's something we're constantly trying to get our babies to do more of. Thoughts about and plans for sleep can consume your life when your child is a baby.

Common Concerns

When you are not actually trying to get your baby to sleep, you're probably wondering about a slew of sleep-related questions: How much sleep will the baby get this time, and will I get any sleep, too? Is he getting enough sleep? Is he sleeping too much? Why is it so hard to get him to sleep? Should I wake him up if he continues to sleep longer than I expected?

Sometimes—and this is psychically painful—you have the opportunity to sleep but can't because you're overtired and you're worried about ever getting a full night's sleep again. Round and round go the worries and the exhaustion, for weeks or even stretching into months.

As if that weren't enough, you notice that questions about your child's sleep habits are almost as common as asking what your baby's name is, with a "That's great!" if your answer meets the questioner's approval or a litany of advice if it doesn't. It's almost as if the age at which your child sleeps through the night is somehow a report card on your parenting.

Babies Are Sleep Minimalists. Or Are They?

Most of the time, when you really add up the hours, the baby sleeps a lot, just in small increments. The only thing you do know is that the baby is getting far more sleep than you are, and that sleep is obviously of some quality if the baby's ability to fuss and cry with great vigor is any indication.

SHEKNOWS SECRET: If you add up the hours, the baby sleeps quite a lot, but, it seems, never long enough for you to get that deep, restorative sleep that you need.

I think we all have ideas of how we'll get our babies to sleep in the early days, but the truth is you use whatever method works. Rocking, swinging, front carriers, or stroller rides— the very first days are all about figuring this little creature out. Once a pattern emerges and is somewhat consistent, you can look at making a series of incremental changes that will move you and your baby toward her falling asleep in a way you deem preferable.

SHEKNOWS YOU'RE NOT GETTING ANY SLEEP

Of course, all babies are different and each baby will vary in her habits from day to day, but as a rule newborns will need to eat every three hours *at a minimum*. And that, alas, includes in the middle of the night (expect a 2:00 A.M. and 5:00 A.M. feeding—yawn). Again, this is a generalization, but sometime between eight and twelve weeks, you can expect your baby to start bunching up feedings and sleep into something of a workable pattern. Also be alert for cluster feeding, an indication that your baby is going through a growth spurt. It can feel like you're feeding your baby around the clock! This is frustrating, but completely normal. Infants typically hit their first growth spurt between seven and ten days old, then again at three weeks, followed by six weeks, three months, six months, and nine months.

Find out more about baby sleep and breastfeeding on our P&B blog: *http://PregnancyAndBaby.com/blog/baby-sleep* and *http://PregnancyAndBaby.com/category/breastfeeding/*.

Sleeping Through What Night?

Almost as soon as your child is born, people will start asking you if he has slept through the night. This is one of the most ridiculous questions anyone can ask a new mother. Of course the baby isn't sleeping through the night—and what does that mean, anyway? There's no magic number that all pediatricians and experts agree on; there's no definitive age at which every child should do exactly the same thing. There are, instead, guidelines.

Every Child Is Different

Every child is unique; every child is wired just a little bit differently. Every child is sensitive to light and sound in a different way. Some are very light sleepers from the start and some are very deep sleepers; some have an easier time of releasing the stimuli of the day than others; and some just reach that developmental milestone sooner rather than later. Some sleep better when they have a full belly; some just seem to need to get to a certain size threshold before they can manage those extra stretches.

SHEKNOWS SECRET: There's no exact, magic number of hours of sleep that means sleeping through the night, or months of age when babies "should" sleep through the night.

Sleeping through the night is not the same for a baby as it is for us. Your child is not going to suddenly sleep for eight to ten hours at a stretch. Developing the ability to sleep that long is a process, for both of you. And you can get pretty worn down and worn out in the process. Some days, the baby just sleeping one extra hour between feedings overnight can constitute through the night. Really, that's all.

"There never was a child so lovely but his mother was glad to get him asleep." —Ralph Waldo Emerson

It Will Happen! (Eventually)

If and when your baby sleeps for about six hours at a stretch, and in the overnight hours, you have yourself a good sleeper.

Take it for what it is and be thankful. Please, for the sake of any mothers around you who might still be struggling, try not to brag about this. Be kind to the sleep-deprived ones among your circle; telling another mom how much your baby sleeps when hers isn't sleeping anywhere near that long is just plain cruel, and you'll have a crying grownup on your hands in addition to your infant.

The ability of a baby to sleep in longer stretches builds over time. It really will happen . . . eventually. It rarely, if ever, happens all at once. It's an extra fifteen minutes here or there, then suddenly you realize she's been asleep a whole hour longer (and you're kicking yourself because you could have been napping or reading in that time, but you were sure she was going to wake up any second, so what was the point?). It's waking up for a feeding and realizing the light outside the window is dawn and your baby slept through the usual 4:00 A.M. feeding.

"I managed to survive college, law school, and the bar exam without ever pulling an all-nighter. Getting sleep has always been a priority for me. It wasn't until I had a newborn that I learned how little sleep I could get and still function (barely)." —Katherine A.

For months, actually, I considered the longer stretches my son would sleep as a gift not to be depended on. Slowly, slowly we realized that our son really was sleeping through the night—well, six hours at a stretch—and we were somewhat functional. We didn't dare say it too loud, though. The sleep gods might have gotten angry and taken it away.

Method or No Method?

Talking with other people about your child learning to go to bed and sleep better is like walking a minefield of opinions, irrational declarations, suggestions of this method or that, and individual defensiveness.

SHEKNOWS SECRET: There is no one-size-fits-all sleep solution.

It seems everyone has advice for how to make it happen. Ask a group of moms on a playground about their method to get their babies to sleep and you'll likely hear as many "methods" as there are moms (including a few well-known physician names or book titles) and plenty of conflicting advice. For every "You must!" there is a "You should never!" These declarations are as much about validation of personal choices as helping you. Actually, more about personal validation. How great for these moms that they figured out a sleep method that works for their family, or mostly works for their family, or whatever! It may or may not work for yours.

"My first and only rule about having a baby when I was pregnant was not letting our baby sleep in our bed. We broke that rule the first day we brought our daughter home. I never made any rules after that." —Karen W.

What Are the Methods, Anyway?

The most popular sleep methods seem to come down to variations on two major themes:

- **Crying it out:** Attempts to teach the baby to self-soothe, usually letting the baby cry for a longer time each session or night
- **Soothing:** Attempts to lull the baby to sleep by rocking, singing, and so on

No matter which way you lean, you have to choose the method (or the hybrid method) that feels right for you, both intellectually and in your gut. And what's right for you and your family may change over time. Trust your instincts and communicate honestly with your partner about what you think is working or not working.

You may think you need to subscribe to some official method or doctor or child-development expert—celebrity sleep coaches certainly can be enticing—but do you really need it? You already have the skills to help your baby get to sleep; you just need to listen to the voice that is telling you those skills.

Keep Things in Perspective

Some people will claim that if you use the method opposite to what they recommend, you'll permanently harm your kids. I had people tell me that by soothing my son to sleep I'd ruin his chances of ever being able to fall asleep on his own. Ever.

SHEKNOWS SECRET: Kids don't have to learn every lifetime skill in the first year.

Um . . . no, I don't agree with that at all. I know plenty of parents who used each of these methods, and as far as I can tell, none of their kids is an ogre. I'm pretty sure mine aren't either. Soon enough, as the kids got a little older, we helped them learn to fall asleep on their own (with many fewer tears), and they all sleep great now. They all fall asleep on their own in their own beds and they stay there; we didn't ruin them forever after all.

Crying It Out Versus Fussing

There is a difference between the crying-it-out methods and having a baby fuss a little before he falls asleep. Particularly if you are having a tough night with bedtime (and those happen no matter what sleep method you choose), letting your child fuss for a few minutes in a safe place while you regroup is not a horrible thing. Maybe you are the one having a bad day and your baby feels your stress or maybe the baby was overstimulated by evening visitors. Stepping away for a few minutes to take some deep breaths and restrategize can be a good thing; it can bring you back to the sleep routine with clearer focus.

Training Versus Learning

The phrase "sleep training" is often used when discussing various sleep methods. That can sound a little . . . rigid. What if you were to think of it as more of an interactive thing, more like sleep learning than training? "Training" sounds like it has a finite beginning and end; "learning" is an ongoing process and more fluid. There will be things that come along in your baby's life that will impact sleep, and learning to deal with variations in life may help sleep become more consistent and comfortable and less of a stress for both of you.

SHEKNOWS SECRET: Think of getting your child to sleep as more of an interactive experience for the two of you; more like sleep learning than sleep training.

The Benefits of a Bedtime Routine

Developing and maintaining a consistent bedtime routine for your child—and yes, even for a baby—is an important part of sleep learning. Routines are like signals to your child: now is the time for play, now is the time for sleep, and so on.

It sounds so obvious, but it can be hard to remember that your baby really needs this routine every night, not five out of seven nights. She's still learning, and she still needs the consistency; she doesn't understand weekends.

SHEKNOWS SECRET: Experts tend to agree on the importance of a bedtime routine to help prepare the mind and body for sleep.

While sleep experts can't all agree on what constitutes an appropriate sleep method, they do tend to agree on the importance of regular routine to help prepare the mind and body for sleep. Infancy may seem too early to introduce a routine, but it's not. If you want reading to be part of your child's bedtime routine, start early with board books for just a few minutes at a time. If you'd like specific music involved, start playing it at bedtime now. Soon enough, your child will get the clue that book time followed by music time is followed by sleep time. With online music services, you can create your perfect bedtime playlist of soothing music (that isn't cloyingly saccharine so you will be able to tolerate it) for your child's bedtime for years to come.

Some babies and children respond really well to light routine; some seem to need it more and more consistently than others. Some kids will tolerate variations to the routine well, but others will struggle if one thing is out of place. You won't really know until you establish a routine and then try to vary it.

Be Flexible

While consistent routine is important, consistent doesn't necessarily mean rigid. If you choose somewhat fluid elements, the routine can be transportable, and that's really helpful for travel. Books and music and blankets and stuffed frogs travel well; specific lamps or paintings on the wall don't.

If a part of your sleep routine isn't working, you can change it. Routines are not inflexible schedules and are rarely perfect the first time, or even the fifteenth time; they necessarily need to evolve as your child gets older. Just because you do it one way when your child is a baby doesn't mean you have to keep doing it that way when your child is four or five.

Cosleeping

Often as big an issue as the sleep method you use or whether your baby has slept through the night, is where the baby sleeps. Cosleeping is becoming more popular, but it is by no means widely accepted. Some pediatricians are fine with it; others are vehemently opposed. Some grandparents will be horrified while others will ask what the big deal is. Some sleep experts think it's fine, some think it borders on child abuse (really!).

The Reasons Behind It

Discussing the topic of cosleeping can feel like a no-win situation, and one of those topics you broach tentatively with those around you. As with other issues, there are advantages and disadvantages to both crib and cosleeping.

"Always kiss your children goodnight—even if they're already asleep." —H. Jackson Brown, Jr.

Some moms just need to have their child physically separate from them while sleeping, whether a crib in the same room or down the hall. It's a personal level of separation. Cribs that adhere to national safety guidelines that are not overfilled with bedding and other stuff (and stuffed stuff) are a very safe way to achieve this. Your child has a safe place to sleep and you have your body to yourself for a bit.

Some moms, though, like to have their babies close by so they stay attuned physically to their baby. Especially for nursing moms (since breastfed babies need to eat more frequently), not having to get out of bed to nurse can feel like a huge benefit and results in less disruption for everyone.

Safe Cosleeping

Just as cribs need to meet safety standards, cosleeping needs to adhere to some safety rules. While many moms report being so attuned to their child that they don't even move in the night, alcohol and drugs or medications can dull this sensation. It takes an honest sense of self-awareness to recognize when cosleeping might be less than absolutely safe for you and your baby, and a willingness to take steps to make sure you are being as safe as possible. Even if you cosleep, don't get rid of the crib just yet.

Some baby-gear manufacturers have started to produce side-sleeping arrangements that attach to the parents' bed to give a kind of hybrid experience: The baby is close by but still has a little space of her own. While only you can decide if this approach will be right for your family, these products can give you some of the benefits of both approaches.

Worries Can Keep Baby Up at Night

Even if your child is a great sleeper, there will still be a tough night or two ahead. Just when you get used to more sleep, along comes a developmental burst or an illness to throw it all into flux.

Approaching a Developmental Milestone

If your child's sleep is suddenly disrupted but she seems healthy, she could be frustrated by her attempts to conquer a developmental milestone. When my son was about nine months old, his sleep started to be very disrupted. It was about the time he was on the edge of crawling, and I sensed the two were related. Then one night, about three in the morning, I felt something whapping me on the chest. There was my son with a big grin on his face, up on all fours right next to me, wanting to show me how he had just figured out how to crawl. He'd crawled over from his cosleeper that was attached to our bed to show me his new skill. After congratulating him quietly and getting him back to sleep, our nights returned to "normal." This is all to say that a few nights of interrupted sleep do not necessarily indicate a sleep disorder or other major sleep issues or a need for sleep re-training.

An Illness Coming On

In some children, sleep disruptions can also indicate the beginning of a cold or ear infection. These situations can be guilt inducing. "I should have seen that coming," you might think or "Why didn't I know?" Every single mom I know has missed an emerging illness at one time or another—and felt guilty about it. But it happens, and it's impossible to have all the answers all the time. Sleep can be affected by so many other things that it's hard to know what is causing the issue, until the issue makes itself absolutely clear.

"How we sleep is also a cultural matter, and how we decide to approach it is a personal one. As for 'good habits,' well, that's your opinion of what a good habit is. . . . If it works for you, more power to you! Parents need a certain amount of sleep to function properly, and only you can decide what that is . . . and then work out something humane with your baby." —Polli K.

Foundation for a Lifetime . . . Kinda

Sleep is such an important part of our lives from infancy through adulthood and affecting mood, learning, and more that we talk a lot about setting a foundation for a lifetime. While that's true in some senses, it doesn't mean that you can't make a change if needed. It can be easy when you want validation for your own choice to say, "If you don't let your kids cry it out, your kids will never be able to fall asleep on their own" or "If you let your kids cry it out, they'll never be truly connected to you." But neither of those statements is wholly true.

There are all sorts of solutions out there. Whichever you choose—cry it out or comfort to sleep, family bed or crib, celebrity sleep-coach advice or gut instinct, rigid routine or almost none at all—it's up to you to decide what is right for your family. And if everyone is getting the sleep they need and is functional, criticisms are just sour grapes.

SHEKNOWS SECRET: Your child *will* sleep—and you will sleep again.

CHAPTER 10

Good Parenting Is Sexy

Imagine your romantic ideal. Go ahead, try it. Imagine what that person looks like; imagine a person so physically attractive you almost swoon, someone oozing sex appeal, whatever it means to you. Now imagine that person being not so nice to a baby or child. Suddenly the romantic ideal isn't so sexy, is it? Suddenly it's just a good-looking person, not necessarily a wholly attractive one, or even remotely attractive in some cases.

Now think about the parents you see around you in your community. The mom who clearly is having a blast on the swings with her son or the dad who is tickling his daughter's belly and they are both laughing so hard there are tears in their eyes. These parents may be physically attractive in very traditional ways, or they may not be. Did you even notice? Does it matter what they look like?

It's What's on the Inside

What is really attractive about these parents is their parenting. Their attentive and engaged parenting is what makes them beautiful, the way they unashamedly give themselves to their children. It even makes them sexy.

Yes, good parenting is sexy. It really and truly is. Give me a balding, slightly overweight good dad over a magazine-cover misogynist any day of the week. Better yet, give me my own husband—a truly great dad.

SHEKNOWS SECRET: Becoming a parent alters all your relationships, especially the one you have with your partner.

Becoming a parent is, of course, life altering. It alters not only you, but your relationships as well—every last one of them. Navigating your romantic relationship amid your new title as parents can be tricky. The attention you and your partner gave each other before and during pregnancy and even right through delivery was intense and focused on each other, even as you planned for and experienced the arrival of your baby. But the moment that baby is born there is something between you, even more literally than when your belly was growing, and definitely figuratively. It links you forever, yet if you are not careful and attentive to the foundation of your romantic relationship, the stress can tear your relationship apart. You can talk Mars and Venus all you want—here on Earth, a new baby is your own personal earthquake.

Who Comes First?

At a wedding rehearsal once, the wise pastor leading the ceremony spoke of loyalties. He said that until the marriage vow is made, one's loyalties are with one's parents. But the moment the marriage vows are made, the loyalties are to the spouse first and to the children of that union second.

For years, I thought about those remarks in terms of spousal and in-law relationships, which is all good and well. But as soon as I had a child of my own, I wondered how to achieve that goal of spouse loyalty first when we had a helpless creature totally dependent on me. Didn't I need to put this baby first, at least for a while?

"What I love most about my husband as a dad is that he jumps right into parenting, never complains if he is tired or the kids are whining, uses humor to diffuse situations, and is a truly great role model." —Kellie B.

It is extremely difficult, if not impossible, to prioritize a healthy and capable adult above a vulnerable, helpless infant. So don't. That's where the difference between loyalties and priorities comes in.

Loyalties Versus Priorities

Loyalty is faithfulness, constancy, devotion. Loyalty is more a sentiment. Sometimes it's an action, too, but it's an emotional feeling of commitment to your partner and the family you are building together. Priority is almost all action, however. It's doing what needs to be done in the order in which it needs to be done.

"The best security blanket a child can have is parents who respect each other." —Jan Blaustone

You can be completely loyal to your partner while putting your baby first in the physical priority line much of the time. In fact, you *are* being loyal to your partner when you do so. By being an attentive and responsive mother, you are showing your commitment to the family you and your partner have chosen to build. Likewise, your partner shows that same loyalty when he shows his understanding of priorities, whether it be doing something directly for the baby or supporting you in what you need to do for the baby. And the baby? The baby isn't asking anyone to choose between this or that or him or her; the baby is just hungry.

SHEKNOWS SECRET: With some mutual understanding, you can be completely loyal to your partner while putting your baby's needs first.

Can You Do It All? No.

In times of sleep deprivation and new-parent insecurity, things can get confused. Even when you need to put the baby first, your partner still has needs and you do, too. Trying to meet everyone's needs at once can feel like, and can be, an exercise in futility.

After the first flush of joy and connection when the baby is born, the first weeks and months of a child's life are often a blur. The feedings, diaper changes, fussing, and sleep deprivation run every parent down. It can be too easy to lose touch with one another in this time; too easy for each parent to feel somewhat neglected and at the whim of this demanding little creature you managed to create.

How to Adjust to Change: Communicate

Women aren't the only ones who redefine themselves as they become mothers. Men or other parental figures do, too. Suddenly, the parents are just that—parents, not Jack or Jill or wife or husband or daughter or partner or son, but mom or dad, and collectively, parents. As much as you have thought about it during the pregnancy, now that it's here, it's different. Whether it's a little different than you thought or a lot different depends on your specific situation.

The baby stuff consumes your waking moments; finding five minutes to communicate about this adjustment—or even just thirty seconds to acknowledge that your partner, the other parent in all of this, might be feeling some big emotions—can go a long way to keeping that connection through the very difficult early days. It can also be very difficult to find those five minutes, much less the right words.

"My hubby had to learn to be a step-parent before he learned to be a parent. Patience is still something he struggles with after all these years." —Ellen S.

Even the best of communicators may have trouble doing this, and may need to learn some new communication skills to muddle through. "I miss you" can convey as much emotion and tenderness as "I love you and I need you" and definitely needs to be heard as often as "Can you hand me that box of wipes?"

SHEKNOWS SECRET: It's okay to miss your old life as a couple.

New parenthood may help you appreciate the time you had alone together, even if it's in retrospect, and make the best of all future one-on-one time you will have. Yes, you will have couple time again.

Parenting Goals and Biases

Even if you and your partner are good communicators (or used to be before parenthood), it can be tough to talk about parenting. We each come to the role with biases from our own experiences, both good and bad. Some new parents may only have a strong idea of how they don't want to parent; the partner can bring to the table what is possible. Some new parents may have strong role models that they want to emulate.

"All my girls have very loving dads—my second husband is very funny and inspires humor in everyone; my first husband is just good with kids. My second husband is mostly a good partner, although sometimes I feel like I have three kids in the house, not two. He does tend to be a little too fun at bedtime . . ."
—Debby S.

Talking about what kind of parents you want to be—for your child and for each other—is worth the effort. It can shine light on differences of philosophy and approach that need to be resolved, and the sooner the better.

Talking about your goals as parents may be very different from practicing those ideals. Working together can help you avoid pitfalls and disagreements and maintain respect for each other as partners and as parents in the middle of an issue. It's impossible, though, to talk about every possible scenario; you just don't know what parenting will bring until you are in it!

SHEKNOWS SECRET: It's okay if you and your partner don't agree on every last aspect of parenting. Communicate often and respect each other's opinions.

Each parent has to figure out his or her own parenting style. Neither of you will do things exactly the same way. As long as it's not actually harmful to your child, allowing one another to parent in their own way (difficult as it may be some days!) shows respect for each other, and you might even learn something new.

Compassion Goes Both Ways

Misunderstandings and disagreements between new parents—even just the feeling of loneliness—can be exacerbated by the physical and emotional tiredness that comes with a new baby. As a mom, you want some compassion for what you are experiencing emotionally and physically (recovery from birth is no picnic), and you deserve that. But your partner deserves some compassion, too—you deserve it from each other.

"Like all parents, my husband and I just do the best we can, hold our breath, and hope we've set aside enough money for our kid's therapy."
—Michelle Pfeiffer

Remembering that you are not the only parent going through this tremendous adjustment—and actually saying that you remember that—is just one of the ways you acknowledge that dads (and partners) need emotional support as parents, too. It's not just new moms who are trying to figure all this out, and you have a lifetime of continuing to try to figure it out, so it does no good to alienate each other now.

SHEKNOWS SECRET: Be sure to recognize that dads (and partners) need emotional support, too.

Toward Becoming Coparents

The little bits of compassion, the discussions about parenting roles, remembering to be friends and partners as well as parents . . . these are all the things that build a couple into coparents for a family. They are also difficult to remember when the new roles feel a bit tough. What coparenting means to you and your partner is going to be unique to your family and your relationship. Dividing up responsibilities, often a first step, is only part of it.

It's virtually impossible to split all the parenting tasks down the middle, but you do need to spread the responsibility around. If you are breastfeeding, you could pump milk so your partner can have the opportunity to feed the baby. Maybe dad does all the nighttime diaper changes and mom does all the daytime changes.

SHEKNOWS SECRET: Don't look for a 50-50 split of responsibilities, but be sure each of you is carrying a fair load.

The point is sharing—a concept you're going to have to help the baby learn eventually—and letting one another find their own best way to do things. Maybe you don't change a diaper exactly the same way your partner does. That doesn't mean that one way is better than the other (maybe it is, maybe it isn't); they are just different. Maybe you can each learn something. Having a little respect for the different ways each of you parent can help you identify the ways you are already compatible as parents.

"I had major issues with my son's father as we were no longer a couple. I felt severe anxiety about having him in my life at all. He and I fumbled through the infant years somehow and once we got past the emotional part of our breakup, we became good friends and good coparents." —Angie T.

Striving to become coparents, in whatever way that means for you and your partner, is one of the ways you can maintain the foundation of your relationship. And when that foundation is solid, it's easier to spark. Suddenly, the way your partner so gently lays down your sleeping daughter after rocking her to sleep could just be the sexiest thing you've ever seen.

Start Dating Again

As the weeks and months of a baby's life pass, hopefully the routine becomes more and more predictable. You may long for your old life, the time when you and your partner could eat an entire dinner without an urgent vocal interruption or didn't have to eat in shifts, one eating while the other held the baby. You may start to think about a way to make it happen again. This is a good urge, a normal urge. Go for it!

Depending on your familial support or babysitter situation, you may be able to create just this opportunity. Your baby will survive a short stretch without you. You may be able to time the outing so you don't even miss a feeding if you are breastfeeding! Even if it's just an hour for you and your partner to have an ice cream together, do it.

How do you and your partner stay connected?

- "Date night." —DEBBY S.
- "Communication and respect." —KAREN W.
- "Ritualized Friday-night takeout, after the kids were in bed. It gave us a break, and something to look forward to, even if we had to eat it late." —LAUREN D.

The first time you and your partner have any kind of a date, don't be surprised if all you can talk about is the baby. It's been your sole focus, so what else is there to talk about? Other conversations, other topics will make their way back into your lives. Give it a little time, but keep at it.

SHEKNOWS SECRET: A takeout picnic on the living room floor or sharing a gourmet cupcake from a favorite bakery can be as romantic and sweet as an actual dinner or dessert out.

Besides an actual out-of-the-house date, you can find ways in your everyday life—even with the demands of the baby—to reconnect. Resolve to spend just five minutes a day together doing anything from talking about what was good in each of your days to doing a puzzle together to just about anything.

Building Family Time

Along with maintaining your romantic relationship, building the whole family dynamic is important, too. Even with a small baby, you can start to create times and events that will provide a framework for family focused time for years to come.

Being a parent as well as a partner is a learning curve for both of you. A baby changes everything, and you both need to learn to give and receive love in different ways with this new baby in the house. Some days, it will all seem to flow naturally and other days will feel harder. Whenever you doubt how it's going, watch your partner as a parent. Watch them—catch them—being more tender and loving than you ever knew possible. Your partner was never sexier.

CHAPTER 11

The First Birthday Milestone

It's as big a milestone for you as it is for your baby. No, scratch that—it's bigger for you. Your baby—not so much a baby anymore—isn't even going to remember this day, even with the copious number of pictures you take. It's a reason to contemplate, a reason to reminisce, and a reason to celebrate. It's a major milestone for the whole family.

Oh, Baby! You've Changed!

A year ago, you and your child were total unknowns to each other. Your personalities were unknown to each other, as were your faces and your touch. Everything was new and different, for both of you.

Your baby was an eating, sleeping, pooping, crying lump, a human in the making—and who knew that a cry that sounded more like a wailing cat could so completely turn you inside out? Every day was a new challenge. Would a routine emerge today? Would your baby sleep enough so you could get a shower?

Within a few weeks, a personality started to emerge. Did your baby show signs of going with the flow or was he Mr. Instant Gratification? Was there colic? What music soothed your baby when he was fussy? When the weeks turned to months, your baby became more and more interactive: belly laughs and definite likes and dislikes and, thankfully, slightly more consistent sleeping. There were the introductions to the high chair and slowly, slowly to solid food. And to real play.

"After a long hard year it was pure celebration, that both he made it and I made it! We all threw these huge parties—we rented out the clubhouse at our condo and had tons of people. For my second and third children, it was a cake and family!" —Kellie B.

There's that lovely age when they are sitting up on their own and playing with things for a minute or two at a time, yet not quite mobile. When you could grab the ringing phone just beyond your reach of him without fear that he'd take off in a crawl down the hallway faster than you could say, "I'll call you right back."

Before you could get used to that stage, your little guy started pulling himself up—and pulling things down! Nothing was safe! You thought you addressed those babyproofing issues, but nope. Every baby is unsafe—and challenges the babyproofing—in their own way. You learn this the hard way. Just when you would get used to one developmental stage, your child would move on to the next one, leaving you in the dust and scrambling to figure out what just happened.

Finally, finally your baby is starting to try to communicate with you. He watches the way your mouth moves when you talk and tries to imitate you, confident the sounds coming out of his mouth mean something to you. Maybe you've taught him baby signs and he can tell you that he wants more of that mango yogurt.

"We had cake in the park with family. It was a few days after my sister-in-law got married, so we were surrounded by family. It was great. My daughter just wanted to eat strawberries." —Karen W.

You're Not the Same Woman You Were

Your baby has changed in so many obvious ways, and so have you. But there are probably other changes in you that are less obvious. People around you can see some of those changes, but they can't see the changes in your heart and soul.

Sure, your body changed, boomeranging belly and all, but so did your whole identity! You're not "just" you anymore. You are so much more than that; you are somebody's mother. In addition to still being you, of course.

"Our birthdays are feathers in the broad wing of time." —Jean Paul Richter

A year ago, as much as you thought you were prepared or as prepared as you could be for your child's birth and for parenthood, the reality of it likely threw you for one big loop. Are you at all the parent you thought you would be a year ago?

SHEKNOWS SECRET: The very first birthday isn't just about the one who was born on the day; it's about the one who gave birth on the day, too.

When your baby was born, you likely knew the basics of baby care in general, but this baby, this personality was different. How quickly did you throw out all your prebirth declarations of how you would do it this way or that way and it would be perfect? A week? Six weeks? Four months?

You gained confidence through the year. You could differentiate your child's cry from other babies, and could figure out quickly whether it was an "I'm hungry" cry or an "I don't know where I am" cry. You didn't even know how you knew which was which, but you did.

Celebrate in Your Own Way

Celebrating your child's first year of life and your first year as a mother doesn't have to be a blowout blast to be momentous and important for you. It should be noted, and whether that noting is an external expression of joy or an internal feeling of relief is wholly up to you.

"Most of us can remember a time when a birthday—especially if it was one's own—brightened the world as if a second sun has risen." —Robert Lynd

Different cultures have different customs associated with a child's first birthday. In some cultures, it's a large celebration; in others, it is more subdued. The celebration is more about the adults than it is the birthday child in terms of menus and activities and decorations. Whether you choose to have a bash with extended family and friends or keep it simple, taking time to consider the emotional import of the day is more important than the cake or the gifts. Celebrate your baby's first year of life, your first year as a mother, and toast to a long, healthy, and happy future for both of you.

Part III
YOUR CHILD

CHAPTER 12

The Mommy Mafia

Women. We are one another's best friends and worst enemies, and that odd hybrid, frenemies. We support and criticize, encourage and judge, comfort and demean. We hold each other up as ideals and tear each other down as failures. We do this to one another on a daily basis. But we definitely don't like to admit it. And we are the worst toward one another over parenting issues.

Judgment Day

Just like the world expands for your child as he grows into a toddler and then a child, so does a mommy's world expand. And when your world expands, you may notice things you hadn't before, like the attitudes and actions of other moms and women around you.

Many moms feel that no matter what they do, they are being judged—and harshly—by just about everyone around them, and especially by other moms. That's because they *are* judging you. No matter what you do, there is someone watching you with a critical eye. It's part jealousy, part competition, and part insecurity—and totally unhelpful, annoying, and even destructive.

Being Judged

The lady in the produce department looking at what's in your cart? Judging you.

Your cousin, when you don't do something exactly the way your shared grandmother did it? Judging you.

Yup, maybe even your mom over any number of things. Judging you—even as she's loving you, too. Anyone who says, "It's not my place to judge, but . . . " is judging you and anyone in her path. It's the dirty little secret that's not so secret.

. . . And Doing It Yourself

You probably do some of that judging of other moms, too. Yeah, you do. I certainly do, even though I like to say I don't. If that other mom doesn't do this, that, or the other thing like you would do it, you judge. Is it better than how you do whatever it is? Worse? And if it is better, does she think she's better than you? We hold constant referendums on each other's choices, intentionally or not.

SHEKNOWS SECRET: No, judging isn't fair. But you know you do it, too.

It's like we moms can't help it. We're constantly looking for validation for the way we have chosen to parent, and we look for it in other moms and how they parent, though that's probably one of the last places we should look! We try not to judge, but it seeps in. Even that kindest, most well-intentioned, supportive, and confident mom has moments of not-so-kind, not-so-well-intentioned, and not-so-supportive thoughts. Even when we try hard not to judge, a thought floats by, bouncing around your ear and suggesting in the tiniest way that maybe you could do it better.

"I love my job so much that I'd always assumed work would continue to be as important to me. But I don't want to miss a second with Violet. Even this morning, leaving her in her high chair going 'Mama! Up, up!' I had to tear myself away. I'm certainly not the first person to feel that way about her child—and she doesn't care if I work. I'm the one who misses her like a love-struck teenager." —Jennifer Garner

Why Do We Do It?

What does that make us, as a whole, as moms? The Mommy Mafia. Enforcers of local social structure and norms, judgers of all who dare to do things differently, and deniers of jealousy when someone else does do it better or experiences some awesome thing—and don't you forget it. Sheesh, that sounds awful. And it is.

SHEKNOWS SECRET: We all come to parenting with the sum of our personal experiences, and each of those experiences is vastly different.

The Mommy Mafia takes many forms, from judging how your neighbor throws a birthday party to how a mom in your playgroup disciplines her child to criticizing a decision to get a part-time job. It invades everything.

Martha Stewart Doesn't Live Next Door

Whether it's child rearing or home keeping, no one does it perfectly. No one. Some are just better at presenting a specific appearance to the outside world. That's all.

I bet there's a mom in your neighborhood that seems to do everything perfectly, a super mommy of sorts. Someone for whom being an everyday superhero (because all moms are superheroes!) isn't enough; she needs to be the superhero's superhero. Or at least that's how it seems. A well-decorated, always-clean house, tidy and polite children, creative entertaining for every event from the weekly playgroup to her child's stunningly coordinated birthday party, maybe even an interesting career on a star-catching trajectory, and plenty of other "perfect" things complete the scene.

Heck, maybe this mom is you. That's great that this mom can do all of that. I wish I could manage it, but I can't. I've entertained daydreams of doing it all, but they remain dreams. Perfection is not going to happen in my life.

"In my opinion, the 'professionalization of motherhood' is ruining the stay-at-home-mom (SAHM) experience. The first time I was a SAHM I got caught up in having to be the perfect mom. My second tour as a SAHM I took the opposite approach—I scheduled almost nothing. And I have more fond memories of that year of doing 'nothing' than I do from any other year I've been alive." —Mary Lou B.

When I see this lifestyle-diva wannabe, I wonder, though, what in her life is imperfect? Because something is, nobody is that perfect. Maybe she is terrible at balancing her checkbook. Maybe she doesn't actually cook in that pristine kitchen, just reheats frozen entrée after frozen entrée. Things like that. (And see there? I'm judging!)

SHEKNOWS SECRET: Nobody is perfect. Some people are just better at making the outside world believe that they are.

You may think you feel pressure from such a mom to try to match her pristine bathroom floor, her pretty children, color-coordinated napkins, and custom-printed birthday invitations. Unless those things are something truly meaningful to you and you decide that's where it's important for you to spend your time, it's a lost cause. You'll always be comparing yourself to that mom, while not developing your own supermommy skills to awe and inspire. That other mom isn't putting the pressure on you to do this—you are putting it on yourself. And when you can't do it the same as that mom? Perfect time to lash out in irrelevant judgment. "Yeah, she has those amazing birthday parties for her kids, but I bet her closets are cluttered. It's all for show."

We all have our strengths and weaknesses. We all have our insecurities, too. It's in those insecurities that we lash out at other moms, look at them with that critical eye. It's how that not helpful, not productive culture of the Mommy Mafia is perpetuated.

The Top Mommy Mafia War Topic: Employment

The Mommy Mafia comes out in force—and I mean in force!—on the topic of stay-at-home (SAH) moms versus working-outside-the-home (WOH) moms. If you thought neighborhood moms could get petty over well-done children's birthday parties, you haven't seen anything yet. I'm sure military organizations could learn something about guerrilla warfare from SAH/WOH battles.

Making the Decision to Work Outside the Home

Today, the working world has opened up to women with many new opportunities for career paths and personal growth, and a vast, churning sea of conflict (and rarely civilized debate) about whether a mom should work outside the home. In this debate, women can be the cruelest to one another.

> *"Have other mothers judged me or have I merely felt judged? Parenting feels risky and requires courage—it's easy to think that there is judgment whenever we have to stretch ourselves or make a leap of faith. I've probably judged myself more than anyone else has judged me. (And if that's not true, don't tell me now!)"*
> *—Lauren D.*

Economic reality requires many women to continue paid employment of some kind. Personal choices drive it for other women. Many of those women may feel conflicted about their decision at some time or another. In that insecurity, the WOH/SAH debate gets heated.

When making the decision to work outside the home and how, know that only you can make that choice for you and your family. Only you can set the criteria that will help you evaluate whether it works or not. Only you can know whether the effort you put into finding appropriate childcare and the reduced amount of time you spend with your child and the crazy scheduling will be worth the return. Your parenting experiences shape your decision making in this area as they do in other areas.

SHEKNOWS SECRET: On some level, the SAH moms who feel the need to lash out at the WOH moms are jealous—but good luck trying to get them to admit it.

Working outside the home can seem a cop-out to some moms who stay home, like you are abdicating your maternal responsibility in favor of some unimportant material acquisition or plain greed. Some moms believe that you must be a stay-at-home mom or you should never have had children in the first place if you plan to work full time. They will even call things like full-day kindergarten "free daycare for parents who don't care enough to stay home with their kids." Really! These women—the ones doing the attacking—are the most insecure about their stay-at-home decision. They can't come to terms with their own decision, so they lash out at anyone who made a different one.

Working outside the home is no picnic. Finding quality, affordable, convenient care situations (that have openings) is a challenge in almost every community. Then you have to make sure you are communicating and negotiating with your employer and partner about schedules, priorities, workload, and so on. If your child gets sick, who goes—you or your partner? How do you make up any work you miss? How will the rest of the household and life responsibilities get done? Do you have coworkers who won't understand and will assume you aren't pulling your weight?

Working outside the home does have its rewards:

- Some women feel that having an identity beyond Mom helps them be better parents.
- Some women feel strongly about contributing financially to the family.
- Some women don't have words to describe it, but just like working. And when Mom is happy, happiness does have a tendency to flow out to the rest of the family.

Making the Decision to Stay at Home

Even with work opportunities opening up to women, many make the choice to stay at home with their children full time. But because there are now more choices for women as far as outside employment, the decision to stay at home can be viewed with suspicion by moms who have made a different choice.

Contrary to popular (prebaby?) belief, being a stay-at-home mom is not all bon-bons and playtime. It's hard work. Being the sole physical and emotional resource for a small, mostly nonverbal and definitely irrational being can be trying. As with any other woman or WOH mom, SAH moms have structure and purpose to their days, too—just different structure and purpose.

"I am so very happy and lucky to be able to stay home and watch every moment of my children's growing years. I know it isn't for everyone, and that's what makes us all different! I love it!" —Kellie B.

When making the decision to stay at home and how, only you can make that choice for you and your family. Only you can set the criteria that will help you evaluate whether it works or not. Only you can know whether the effort you put into your days and nights—and possibly into creative budgeting—are worth it.

Staying at home can seem like a cop-out to some moms, like you are abdicating your individuality and intelligence in favor of talking puppets on public television and macaroni-and-cheese cuisine. There are moms who believe that if you have been educated in a certain way or gained some professional level you owe it to yourself and the rest of the world to keep up working outside the home. There are even moms who will denigrate all your choices about being at home. Those are the moms who are most insecure about their own decision to work outside the home.

SHEKNOWS SECRET: On some level, the work-outside-the-home moms who feel the need to lash out at the stay-at-home moms are jealous—but good luck trying to get them to admit it.

Staying at home is no picnic. It can be hard to be home alone with a baby and/or child all day, somewhat isolated and with limited adult contact. Sometimes you may feel like your ability to have a conversation is reduced to "What sound does a cow make?" and "Please eat your chicken nuggets."

Staying at home does have its rewards:

- You get to be with your baby all day! You can make your own schedule and guide his learning and interactions in the way you see fit.
- Some women don't feel the need to have an identity beyond Mom and are fortunate enough (and sometimes creative and

frugal enough) to be able to swing it financially within their families.

- Some women don't have words to describe it; it just feels right to them. And when Mom is happy, it has a tendency to flow to the rest of the family.

The Best of Both Worlds or the Worst of Both Worlds?

Some women try a hybrid approach and work outside the home part time. This can bring many of the benefits of working outside the home *and* staying at home—and all the stresses and drawbacks of both. Including the comments of the Mommy Mafia.

Many women turn to part-time work as a way to assist the family financially and find some self-fulfillment while not being always absent physically. It sounds so good, and in just the right situation, it is good. But just like moms who stay at home full time and moms who work outside the home full time, finding and maintaining the balance is a constant effort.

SHEKNOWS SECRET: No matter what you choose to do, no one is going to hand your solution to you on a silver platter.

From a strictly mommy-support point of view, SAH moms in the community have a ready-made social structure in other SAH moms in the places they frequent around town during the day: the playground, the library, walks, and so on. It is not hard to find other moms in these places. Similarly, WOH moms have a similar structure in place at the locations they frequent: the daycare center, the grocery store at that certain time of day, and so on.

"As I get older, I truly don't give a flying you-know-what. . . . I honestly don't measure myself against other people's choices." —Hadass E.

But what about moms who are part time in each of those worlds? It's much harder to find one another. The part-time-in-each-world moms often have such variations in schedule that finding each other for mutual support and companionship is difficult, and they aren't completely accepted in the SAH *or* WOH social circles. You're not quite what any of them expect; you're a threat to the Mommy Mafia in both camps. Throw in the possibility of not being wholly accepted by the full-time employees at work (and maybe even being expected to do essentially full-time work on part-time hours and part-time pay), and you see that, no matter what, it's never a perfect situation.

SHEKNOWS SECRET: Not being wholly a part of either the SAH social structure or the WOH social structure in your community can mean you feel even more isolated.

Have It All . . . Just Not All at Once

Once you make a decision to be the mom with the superclean house and fabulous birthday parties or the more granola, earth-friendly mom with amazing garden or the supervolunteer mom or the soccer coach mom or the work-outside-the-home mom or the stay-at-home mom or the whatever-it-is mom, is that choice set for the rest of your life? If you figure out that it's not quite working, either in the near term or distant future, are you stuck with your decision? Absolutely not.

> *"I remember feeling terribly guilty for staying home with my new baby. It wasn't an issue concerning work or feeling like I needed to be doing more. No, I felt guilty because I had the most amazing human being to ever grace the face of this planet, and I was selfishly keeping him to myself." —Jen O.*

Instead of thinking about having it all and all at once, what if you think about having it all in sequence? Could you swing being a stay-at-home mom in a couple years, but for now you'll keep working? Then maybe go back to part-time work a few years after that? Or start a new career? If you look at your life as chapters, what comes in the next chapter? How does the plot grow and change?

Granted, thinking about having it all in sequence won't silence the Mommy Mafia raging outside your windows, but could it calm the Mommy Mafia inside you? Would it help you feel more secure in your current decision knowing you can make a change at some point, when the time is right for you?

The Mommy Mafia Within

Whether it is stay at home or work outside the home, perfect appearance or perfect children, or whatever is most important to us individually, it would be nice to feel more supported by other women as we struggle through our own choices, but it's not going to happen until we offer it ourselves. When we are truly happy with our own choices, there is no need to lash out at any other mom and her choices; when we are truly at peace with our own choices, the criticisms of others roll off our very strong backs.

SHEKNOWS SECRET: The way to stop the Mommy Mafia is simple, really: stop participating in it, stop being it, and start giving what we most want to receive.

It turns out the worst of the Mommy Mafia is within. We are not just one another's best friends and worst enemies; we truly are our own worst enemies—when we really need to be our own best friends.

CHAPTER 13

Playgroups Are for Moms, Not Children

Being a mom can be lonely sometimes. Even though you have another person in the room—your child, and maybe your partner—most of the time, you are still doing this parenting thing alone. There's only one mother, and that's you.

We don't exactly share the experience of mothering; we may have very similar experiences, and there may be common themes that run through our days, but when it comes down to it, we mother by ourselves. Even our partners don't quite feel it in the same way. We make decisions ourselves, take responsibilities ourselves, deal with consequences ourselves, and no two parents have quite the same experience with the same situation. That's a sobering thought, really. And it can be isolating.

For Whom the Playgroup Meets

It's in the commonalities of our experiences, the similar (not the same) threads that run through the days of mothers—of parents—everywhere that we can look to one another for understanding and as a way to create a larger bond. In those ways, we are not alone. And to that end, we may look for playgroups.

Playgroups are—well, can be—seminal experiences for new moms. Amongst everything you are learning and doing and becoming, they are a place to relax a little and hopefully receive validation from other moms at similar places in their mothering experience. Yes, we call them "play" groups as if it's all about the children playing together, but they really are all about the moms. The kids may not like each other very much, but if the moms get along famously—or even marginally—the kids will manage and adjust.

Old Circle, New Circles

When you became a mother, when your life changed, your circle of friends may have changed, too. Particularly if you are the first of your girlfriends to have a child, your old friends may not quite understand your new life . . . yet. Those old friends may be thrilled that you have become a mother, may understand intellectually that you can't drop everything and go meet them, but emotionally they may be smarting at the loss of their "old" friend while still waiting to see what new form the friendship will take.

SHEKNOWS SECRET: Sadly, some friendships do not survive this nonparent-to-parent transition and many go through some tiptoeing for a while before the new dynamics are clear.

While such a situation is unfortunate, it's no reason to cast the old friends aside. Better, it's reason enough to find new friends, and preferably new ones who live nearby, have children around the same age, and have a similar open spot on the weekly schedule.

"We were lucky in that even though we were the first of our friends to have kids, everyone else was pretty close to that stage and happy to come over and oogle the little guy. Since I was never a night owl, I welcomed the built-in excuse that the baby provided. No one could pressure me to go out to bars!" —Katherine A.

Mommy Dating

Maybe you thought you were done with dating. Sure, in the traditional sense, this may well be so. Maybe you thought that tentatively getting to know a new person, carefully revealing your own personality, wondering if you could possibly be compatible for the long haul, thinking about what you are wearing, and not eating messy foods early in the relationship were things of the past. Nope.

SHEKNOWS SECRET: Finding a playgroup is a lot like dating—and sometimes under the more critical eye of the Mommy Mafia.

There are nervous phone calls and e-mails, coordinating of schedules, descriptions of your children, light banter about superficial topics, firmer plans, and finally, a meeting. On the appointed day, maybe you even coordinate what you and your child wear—not too casual, dressy, sloppy, frumpy, color coordinated, and so on. Maybe you are anxious to ring the doorbell.

SHEKNOWS SECRET: Finding playgroups is about finding friends for you.

With any luck—and a whole lot of relaxing—you've found a playgroup that you think will work. Maybe you even look forward to playgroup days more than you realized you would. Phew! It really is a relief in addition to a new set of friends.

Some playgroups stay together for years and the moms and kids bond for the long term. While this is rare, indeed fairly special, it does happen. Going into a potential playgroup situation looking expressly for that dynamic, that possibility, puts quite a lot of pressure on what should be a fun interaction for both you and your child.

Finding a Playgroup

While some playgroups are created on an ad-hoc basis—maybe a couple moms in the neighborhood notice an uptick in the number of young toddlers at the local playground and specifically ask some of those moms to join a formal playgroup—others are created through civic and religious organizations. Still others are created through community centers, and some even through medical offices.

> "Friendship doubles our joy and divides our grief."
> —Swedish proverb

Even though you have lived in a town your entire life, organizations geared toward new arrivals in town are often a great place to find playgroups. Some of these organizations may even have dedicated playgroup organizers who can help place you in a playgroup that meets exactly when you have time in your schedule. These groups are often very loose in structure and rotate among the homes of the members. Some such groups put together playgroups on a yearly basis—say, each September. While you can certainly join after that initial formation time, jumping into established interpersonal dynamics can be a challenge.

Churches, especially larger churches, may offer playgroups as a way to interact with other moms who share similar religious values. Depending on how religious you are, this can be something that can bring you a closer, richer experience with your faith-based community. Or not. Everyone has different thresholds for involvement in various community organizations (including churches), and it's okay to maintain boundaries that are comfortable for you.

Playgroups that are formed by and meet at community centers may be more structured than playgroups that meet in homes. There may be fees to attend and there may be weekly educational themes led by a medical or healthcare professional—how your child is developing, physical and emotional changes you may be experiencing as a new mother, and other such topics. These can be fabulous resources, but they are very formal. From these can grow more informal gatherings, but that kind of extra gathering time may take longer to develop based on timing and logistics.

"We had to look around before we found our 'people,' in terms of playgroups. We had a few tries that just didn't feel right. What finally worked for us is when we joined the cooperative nursery school in town—all of our friendships grew out of that, most still last until this day, eleven years later!" —Polli K.

Neighborhood ad-hoc playgroups are going to be a microcosm of neighborhood dynamics—good and bad. Sure, it's a great way to get the scoop on the kookier neighbors and build up a perimeter of people you can call on in an emergency, but it's also a place where the local Mommy Mafia is out in force, and you really have to watch your Ps and Qs, or you'll be the kooky neighbor facing open judgment. Community gossip goes both ways.

Playgroup Politics

After dating playgroups—or even sticking with the first one you tried—you will very quickly notice certain social dynamics among both the moms and the kids.

"For a short time I was a member of a play group that mostly consisted of women who were the wives of doctors at a particular hospital where my mother works. After a few weeks, I couldn't do it anymore—it wasn't that they were cruel or overtly rude to me, but we had nothing in common. I couldn't understand their lives of relative leisure and they couldn't understand my life as a very young working mother. They tended to make me feel guilty about not spending enough time with my son." —Ruth D.

Who's Who in a Playgroup

There always seem to be one or two de facto leaders of a playgroup, whether the playgroup actually needs or wants one or not. These are the ones suggesting this outing or that or declaring that some such toy was the best ever, and you really have to get one for your child. These are the ones that seem to exude confidence—though you probably can't say for certain whether it's true confidence or a well-expressed façade. Is she trying to convince herself as much as anyone about that great toy?

There's usually one much more timid and/or reserved mom in the playgroup. Maybe she's always been quiet or maybe she's having a tougher time adjusting to the demands of motherhood. She's the one I've often found the most interesting. There's a story there, and you may need to work to get it out, but it's very interesting, and she might just give you the support you need beyond the playgroup if you'll do the same for her.

Then there are the in-between moms. The ones who have more obvious good days and bad days, are leaders some days and timid another. They make up the middle of the playgroup pack.

When one mom in the playgroup has older kids and none of the others do, the newer moms constantly asking for advice or quizzing the more veteran mom can create a challenging dynamic. Maybe that veteran mom enjoys having all the answers, but maybe she doesn't; maybe she just wants to hang out on Thursday afternoons, not be the designated community resource for tips and tricks to get the kids transitioned from the crib to the toddler bed.

Just because you are in a playgroup for a while doesn't mean you have to stay in it. Sometimes, it's general group dynamics that push you to make a change and sometimes specific situations trigger a departure. You thought you were long out of high school, right? Not quite.

Welcome Back to High School

In every group of people—whether just women or moms or couples or whatever—there will be specific interpersonal dynamics, specific politics. Not everyone is going to be compatible all the time, and sometimes cliques form. Misunderstandings and conflicts arise, too.

"From swapping parenting tips to a 'no kids allowed' gabfest over martinis, I don't know where I would be without my mom friends. Not only do the kids learn early social skills like sharing, but moms get much-needed adult conversation. I highly recommend finding a playgroup!" —Kim G.

When misunderstandings and conflicts happen within local playgroups, the fallout can feel just like the cruelest days of high school. Women can get mean and defensive and take sides, they can also say things they wish they hadn't minutes later. But there's no principal's office to call for help.

What can be most disturbing about this is that the not-so-wonderful behavior is being observed by the kids. In an era when schools are doing significant work to try to reduce bullying, kids are learning it at home—starting in playgroups when they are very young. If you see this dynamic happening, walk away and find a healthier playgroup community.

Virtual "Playgroups"

If a real-life playgroup just isn't working out, there's always the Internet. While it's not exactly the same experience of sitting and having coffee with girlfriends while the kids whap each other on the heads with plastic toys, finding an online group of moms for support can be extremely rewarding and helpful.

Virtual playgroups aren't constrained by daylight. You don't need to wait for Tuesday afternoon to get a little emotional support for a difficult overnight with a feverish child. (In real life, of course, you wouldn't go to playgroup if you had a feverish child!) And with online friends, someone is almost always online, too. Because virtual mom groups tend to be larger, there is bound to be someone with whom you are compatible. You can stick with your Internet group if you move—instead of having to go through playgroup dating all over again in a new community (unless you want to, of course). While there's less (or no) face-to-face interaction in an Internet-based group, they do at least do away with the pretense that they are for the kids.

If finding a playgroup is like dating, finding an Internet-based group is online dating.

> *"It's the things in common that make relationships enjoyable, but it's the little differences that make them interesting." —Todd Ruthman*

Interpersonal politics can rear their ugly heads in Internet groups just as they can in real life. Sometimes the issues get blown way out of proportion; even when a mom is an excellent writer, misunderstandings can happen, whether by typo or word choice or even the mood of the person reading the post. When feelings are hurt, a face-to-face apology and a hug are still superior, but that just can't happen with Internet groups, so hurt feelings can linger. You may be able to participate in your pajamas (maybe don't turn on the webcam), but you still need to think about how you present yourself and how you respond to others.

SHEKNOWS SECRET: Internet-based groups can go on for years and years, well beyond the typical lifespan of a "real" playgroup.

Some Internet-based groups do meet in real life, or at least some of the moms and kids do. Whether a large group gathering or one mom meeting up with another while the family is traveling through, the relationships can become more than screen and keyboard based; your Internet playgroup can become your real-life playgroup.

CHAPTER 14

Tantrums and the Not-So-Terrible Twos (or Threes?)

Not everybody is going to have terrific twos or terrible threes. Twos might really be terrible and threes might be awesome, or both might be a bit of both. Some parents find both good parts and challenging parts in each age of a child. For example, you might have a kid that has a pretty decent go of things for six months or so after her birthday, then has a harder time in the months leading up to the next birthday—almost every year.

Emerging Personality, Emerging Independence

One of the things that make the toddler years so fun—and sometimes so frustrating—is the emerging personality. You probably had an idea of your child's personality before this, but now it's really settling in. If your child was easygoing as an infant, she is likely still a bit that way; if your child was nicknamed Miss Instant Gratification as an infant, she's likely still wanting things now, now, now.

As they approach the second birthday, toddlers become more and more independent. They've been feeding themselves for a while, but now they are fiddling with clothes, trying to get into things, wanting to do it all themselves. "I do it!" your daughter might cry, and of course there's the classic toddler cry of, "Mine!"

"Two is terrific! Three is when they really make you work. I absolutely love the language acquisition process. You start to glean, through their early words and phrases, how they are interpreting their world."
—Lauren D.

SHEKNOWS SECRET: Two-year-olds are bigger and they know it—but they're not quite big *enough* for some things . . . and that can be frustrating for both of you.

Toddler years are often when the unique family terms and quirks emerge, often as mispronunciations of other words. One of my sons heard the word "careful" as "chareful" ("ch" pronounced like in "chair"). To this day, it's a family word. "Be chareful!" we say to one another. Every family I know has a few of these family terms that get bounced around for years if not decades—one of the ways we hold on to this sweet time.

However, just because toddlers speak better at two or three, you can't expect adult-level reasoning skills from them. Reason for a three-year-old is, "I want it, therefore it should be mine," not, "If Mommy does something for you, you do something for Mommy." *Quid pro quo* just doesn't exist yet. An understanding of cause and effect is developing, but don't count on it to play out in your favor anytime soon.

Managing Expectations

Because of what you've heard, you might dread two—or you might not. You might be steeling yourself for it—or you might decide you won't worry about it until you get there.

> **SHEKNOWS SECRET:** Just because you hear the term "terrible twos" does not mean your child will be terrible at two.

SHEKNOWS THE SIGNS OF AUTISM

What are some signs that your toddler might have autism? Look for: delayed speech, repetitive habits, stacking or aligning objects, a fascination with a certain part of a toy (such as the wheels on a toy car), lack of eye contact, sometimes seems deaf (yet you know he can hear based on other behavior), if a lot of noise or activity can trigger a tantrum, or odd movement patterns (flapping hands, spinning around, walking on tiptoes). However, be sure to realize that a non-autistic child could have any of these behaviors—and a child with autism might have one or none of these characteristics. If you're concerned, please talk to your child's pediatrician. And don't wait; the sooner intervention is started the better chance your little one has to learn and adapt and get the most out of life! For more information on autism, go to www.SheKnows.com/autism.

If you expect two will be terrible, it might become a self-fulfilling prophecy and yes, it will be terrible. Or maybe you'll be pleasantly surprised. Set yourself up for it to be one way or another, and you might miss what it really is: just fine, and just another developmental age and stage. It's an age and stage every child goes through—and has to go through—to get to the other side.

Every age has its challenges, and every child is challenging in a different way. Every age and stage deserves a little research into understanding appropriate and expected development, and with a bit of understanding of that, you may just find that two is terrific. Save the dread for the teen years, when it's really warranted.

What *Was* That?

Your child's first full-fledged tantrum is something of a rite of passage for a parent. It's a sight to behold, the first time your child all-out loses it in a direct battle of wills with you. It's an emphatic collision of desire with reality, with some as-yet-undeveloped psyche sprinkled on top. And it's absolutely developmentally appropriate.

You may wonder how you will know if it's really a tantrum. Oh, you'll know. Don't you worry about that.

The first time my oldest son threw a tantrum, I thought aliens had invaded his body. I remember looking at him, wide eyed, like he was acting out a scene in *The Exorcist*. I have no idea what triggered the tantrum (he was two, did there have to be a coherent reason?), but I remember the scene. For me, it happened in slow motion. I remember every slow blink of my eyelids as I watched my son struggle to manage his emotions.

I was so shocked by what I saw that I froze. I remember comforting him when it was all over, trying to help him understand these huge emotions that were coursing through and overwhelming his little body (he scared himself as much as he shocked me) yet still not giving in to his demands. As loud and demanding as my son could be during a tantrum, it is no match for the stubbornness of his mother.

> *"Parents who are afraid to put their foot down usually have children who step on their toes."*
> —*Chinese Proverb*

I was most concerned about my son having a tantrum in public. What would people think of me? Would they think I was a bad mother? If and when your child has a public tantrum, you still have to parent him through the tantrum. Oh, you may notice one or two overly judgmental observers—and you wish their mothers were there to recount some of *their* toddler tantrums—but there will also be moms who have been there and experienced that. If you're lucky, one will give you a knowing smile, reassuring you that it's normal and it's okay—knowing she's past that phase and thank goodness for that!

Decide on Discipline

If you haven't done so by the time your child is two—and before that first tantrum—it's time to think discipline strategy. You have probably been doing this already to a certain extent, but now it's time to get serious.

SHEKNOWS SECRET: Discipline is not a single act or event, but an ongoing process of learning, for both you and your child.

Discipline is not punishment. Yes, there may be some punitive elements as part of discipline, but through discipline, you want to teach your kids right from wrong, okay behaviors from not-so-okay behaviors, and so on. It's a process.

When You Can't Redirect Anymore

Until now, you've been able to get away with redirecting your child or simply removing him from a situation. Don't want him in your sock drawer? Move him someplace where it's okay to play. That's not going to work so well anymore—and for a while it's likely been working less and less well. Your child has been building on the concept of object permanence since you played that game in the high chair: he dropped something over the side and you picked it up. It still exists! It didn't disappear forever! The sock drawer hasn't disappeared, either.

That concept has only become more and more firm. Self-control, however, is pretty much nonexistent. Sure, you say "No" when you move your son away from your sock drawer, but he knows it's there and wants to go back to it—and tries to. He really can't control himself yet. He has to learn what "No" means when it comes from you (and not just that it's a handy thing to say when he's had enough peas, thanks).

What Is Discipline for Your Family?

Discipline can be a dicey thing, especially intergenerationally and culturally. Dicey to discuss, dicey to implement, and dicey to follow through on. The norms for discipline when we were small are much different from what they are today. While some of this is due to an increased understanding of human—small human—behavior, some of it is cultural, and some of it is situational.

"Twos can mean trouble. I have had to call poison control for each of my kids for something they ate or drank at age two. But my second child wins the prize for a trip to the ER for climbing up into the medicine cabinet and getting into the Tylenol, a 911 call when she put nail polish in her eye, and starting a fire with our kitchen stove." —Mary Lou B.

Discipline is also, often, a very private thing. How you decide to discipline has roots in how you and your partner were disciplined (or weren't, as the case may be) as children as much as it is based on books and advice from your child's pediatrician or other respected people in your life. Also, our children are raised in different environments now, and the situations they and we encounter may be inconceivable to grandparents and great-grandparents.

How each of us disciplines in relation to some of those situations is unique. For example, many of our parents and grandparents didn't use daycare; therefore, learning and thinking about partnering with the discipline policy at school and working in a complementary manner is something they just didn't have to do.

SHEKNOWS SECRET: You will probably not find a one-size-fits-all disciplinary approach—you may have to use several for different situations or for different children.

In addition, not every child can be disciplined the same way. What works for one child may not work at all for another, and may have mixed results for still another. You may have to cycle through a couple of approaches before you figure out what discipline approach is really going to work for you and your family and your situations, and you may have different approaches for different children.

Different Abilities + Different Personalities = Different Discipline

No matter what discipline strategy you use, you must take care to ask for behaviors your child is capable of providing. This goes for every age group from young toddler to teenager. Expecting too much from a two-year-old can be even more frustrating than basic two-year-old discipline issues.

Two-year-olds can't, for example, process the "I do for you, you do for me" concept. For example, "If I give you this ice cream, you have to be good at the supermarket." You can try all you like, but if your child gets the ice cream, that's all that matters to him. If you try to implement and depend on that give-and-take scenario for your two-year-old, you're both going to be frustrated.

SHEKNOWS THE TOP 10 DISCIPLINE ISSUES
Even the most remarkably well-behaved children are going to test your boundaries from time to time. Here are the ten most common discipline issues: rudeness, talking back, not listening, whining, interrupting, teasing, bickering, cheating, lying, and stealing. Most of these issues are going to come up, to some degree. Don't let yourself be blindsided! You'll react with less emotion—and therefore more effectively—if you've taken the time in advance to think about how you'll discipline. You can find our recommended discipline strategies for these ten most common issues at *http://SheKnows .com/articles/4519.htm.*

(In)Consistency

As much as any specific discipline strategy, consistency in message and application of that strategy is key. It sounds obvious, right? Well, it is obvious, but it's not always so easily done.

Inconsistency is a beacon of weakness to a child, even a child as young as two. Children have an uncanny ability to hone in on cracks in the armor and exploit them. If you say that you are going to leave a shop or an ice cream parlor because your child is not doing as asked (and it's something they are capable of doing), if your child doesn't stop, you have to leave. You have to. If you don't, your child gets the signal that you aren't serious and the efforts to exploit that weakness begin.

Similarly, changing discipline strategies midstream, either from punishment to reward or vice versa, will further weaken the front. If you regularly switch to offering some kind of a reward for good behavior after threatening to leave a situation for bad behavior, why should your child ever listen to you the first time? Why should even a two-year-old stop the silliest of little things if his experience is that if he holds out, there's a lollipop on the other end? You can call your child persistent if you want, but as a parent, you owe it to your child to be even more persistent, and consistent.

SHEKNOWS SECRET: Inconsistency is a beacon of weakness to a child, even a child as young as two.

Set Consequences You Can Live With

More than once, I have declared in haste and frustration that if my child did not stop doing something, something else would have to give ("If you don't stop standing on the chair, we're leaving the ice cream store"). Instantly, I regretted it. Of course, in that moment, my child sensed my weakness and did not stop, so I had to show I was a consistent mom and leave.

SHEKNOWS SECRET: Make sure that whatever consequences you offer for a particular behavior, you can endure those consequences, too.

More than a few ice cream cones and trips out that I was looking forward to were cut short due to my haste and lack of thought. And some of those times, the trip to the playground was as much for me to get out of the house as for my son, so taking that away really punished both of us.

Forget about Being Liked

Discipline is not about like, it's about love—your love for your child and your desire to help her grow into a productive member of society. Your child is not going to like you all the time, especially when you are applying discipline. At this young age, with all their emotional immaturity, there will be times when your child won't love you, either.

Separating being liked and loved by your child from discipline is necessary, and difficult. It's nice for all of us to be liked and loved and to feel that affection. Parenting a child is not about what we get back from the child in terms of hugs and kisses, it's about what we can give to them: our unconditional love and guidance and safety. It's part of what we are giving to them when we discipline. We get some of it back, of course, but not all of it.

SHEKNOWS SECRET: If you are thorough and consistent in your approach to discipline, you
can pretty much guarantee there will be times
your child won't like—or love—you. It's completely normal—and they come back around
pretty quickly.

You might like to think that your child is a mirror, and in
many ways, she is. You project love and you get back love. Simple
enough, right? Well, maybe eventually. At this young age (and
for much of childhood, really), the love you shine in may bounce
around inside your child, off slightly askew mirror after slightly
askew mirror. Eventually it will come bouncing back at you, just
not right away. It's kind of like being in an emotional funhouse hall
of mirrors, stretched and shrunk and all over the place.

*"Oh. My. God. My first son had the 'terrible twos'
for about six months; after he could communicate his
needs things were so much easier. Which left me totally
unprepared for my second son, who had the 'terrible
twos' for several years." —Ellen S.*

A United Front

Also critical in discipline is establishing and maintaining a united
front among the parents and any other adults in a position of
authority. If you think kids can sense a crack in your armor and
try to exploit it, just watch them go after an inconsistency between
their parents. You probably remember trying to do this yourself:
playing one parent off the other for personal benefit. Wasn't it fun?

SHEKNOWS SECRET: You and your partner need to agree upon the general discipline approach, understand your individual weaknesses, and maintain a united front.

As with other parenting issues, talking with your partner about your discipline strategy is key. You both need to agree upon the general philosophy you'll use, understand your individual weaknesses, and refine your communication skills over discipline. You also each need to be able to speak up when you think things aren't going well. As with every other parenting issue, if it's not working, change it. Find what does work for you and for your family and do it together.

Positive Reinforcement

During ages when we find our children's behaviors so challenging, it can be easy to slip into very negative patterns of response and effort. Yes, your child needs consistent discipline and sometimes a punitive measure, but they also need to know when they are doing things right, and three-year-olds are increasingly able to do things right. They are learning to truly play with other kids, they are learning about sharing, they are learning what they can do as well as what they can't, and they need consistent reassurance and support for all of that, too.

Catching your child doing something right is such a joy, and balances the days when you feel like everything is going up in flames. Those are the moments to try to etch in your brain, alongside the memory of the breakfast cereal dumped all over the kitchen floor or the day your son got into your new expensive moisturizer and slathered it all over the cat.

SHEKNOWS SECRET: Actively look for things your child does right, and praise her for them.

Telling your child, too, about how proud you are of him for sharing so well or being so nice to someone or putting away his art supplies on his own reinforces the behaviors you want to see for the long haul. Just like you like to be told you are doing a good job as a parent, kids like to be told they are doing a good job as a kid. Be specific!

Terrible or Terrific?

Though not as big as the changes in her first year, your daughter is still going through tremendous developmental transitions. Physically, she is bigger and more agile, her emotions are bigger, and her understanding of the world around her is growing, too. Discipline is one of the ways we teach our children about using their bodies and emotions appropriately in that expanding world.

SHEKNOWS SECRET: Remember, discipline is a process. Be consistent, but try not to dwell on every little misstep she has (there will be plenty!); look at the big picture to see the progress your child is making.

Every child goes through discipline issues. Every child has to learn about the right way and wrong way to act; every child will have missteps, both public and private. It's called being a kid—and we did it, too. Whether it's happening at two or twelve is secondary, it's the same basic, loving guidance process, albeit with different techniques. Every child goes through it, whether you call it terrible or terrific (at any age!) is up to you.

CHAPTER 15

Tales from the Potty

For the first three years of your child's life, you know pretty much everything that goes into—and comes out of—his body. You are the master of input and output.

During the course of this job, you've become more familiar with poop than you ever thought possible, and probably more than you ever wanted to.

I'm sure during this time you've thought to yourself, "I can't wait until this kid is potty trained!" We've all thought that. The final result is wonderful, actually; it's all that it's cracked up to be! But getting to that blissful end-stage of a diaper-free life may take a whole lot longer than you think, with plenty of twists and turns along the way. There even may be moments when you would prefer a diaper over some of the more intense potty issues.

Diaper Drama

When your child is a baby and toddler, you probably didn't give diapers and transitioning to using a toilet much thought. You had the typical issues all parents face, like the occasional diaper blowout at home, the monster blowouts in public (why is it always that way?), and running out to get diapers and/or wipes in the middle of the night.

*"They were all pretty slow. It happened eventually. I
knew they wouldn't walk down the aisle in diapers. No
pressure. It was a bit rough at school with accidents for
my daughter but now she seems to be doing better."*
—Hadass E.

You may have people in your extended family or community
who declare that their kids were trained so much earlier than kids
these days and may even throw in a comment about how it's really
shameful that parents let their kids run around in diapers so long.
Try to ignore these comments, though it can be hard. While there
may be cultural and generational elements to comments about
potty training, circumstances are different!

It's certainly true that diapers, both cloth and disposable, are
more absorbent than they were decades ago, which is both good
and not so good. That means wet or dirty diapers are easier to clean
up than the diapers our parents and grandparents used, but it may
also mean that kids don't feel the wetness on their delicate skin
and respond to that as early as kids (well, we) used to. This may
also mean that when kids start signaling that they are ready to use
the toilet, they are really ready!

Deciphering the Smoke Signals

When do you start looking for the signals? Whenever you think
your child might be ready. The first signals can start long before a
child is really ready to use the potty consistently; many kids use
the potty here and there before complete potty training is in the
realm of possibility. When your child starts communicating that
she has done or is about to do something in that diaper, then it

might be time to start paying attention to the potty issue: potty talk, potty mechanics, basically, all things potty.

SHEKNOWS SECRET: It's time to start introducing all things potty when your child tells you that she is going to or has filled her diaper.

The first step often is just potty talk, and not the kind of yucky potty talk you'll be trying to stop in your children later. It's declaring your family's potty terminology (Pee? Wee-wee? Poop? BM?) and matter-of-fact talk about how we all pee and poop. It's communicating that this function of our bodies is entirely normal, and that we all had to learn how to use the potty when we were little.

What is your advice for potty training?

- "My kids decided when they were ready. No stickers, no bribes, let them lead!" —KELLIE B.
- "Don't rush it, and cloth diapers do help kids know when they are wet." —DEBBY S.
- "Try not to stress. Each kid is different." —KAREN W.
- "If you wait until they are ready, it's a SNAP!" —LYNNE T.
- "Wait until your child is developmentally ready, and either interested or capable of being motivated to be interested." —LAUREN D.

How little is little? Most kids I've known have potty trained somewhere around age three. Some a few months (and even many months) earlier and some a few months (and even many months) later. Potty training can be easy, it can be hard, and it can be all manner of effort in between. It is most definitely not a competition among the kids (well, more accurately, the moms) in your playgroup. It is what it is, and it will all work out in the end. Your child will potty train. She won't go to ninth-grade hockey tryouts in a diaper.

SHEKNOWS SECRET: Potty training is sometimes a long, drawn-out process, but sometimes it's not. Don't let other people's stories scare you; just deal with your own child.

Another Method

Are you tired of parenting "methods" yet? I know I am. There are so many, and so many of them contradict one another! Ask a dozen moms how they potty trained their children, and you'll likely hear a dozen stories of methods and hybrid approaches that eventually led to success—with some small failures along the way.

> *"A child can go only so far in life without potty training. It is not mere coincidence that six of the last seven presidents were potty trained, not to mention nearly half of the nation's state legislators."*
> —Dave Barry

There are how-to books and "guaranteed" methods out there and advice galore. There are "experts" in potty training who might not be experts at all. Be wary of guarantees! Be wary of self-declared experts! That person doesn't know your child!

SHEKNOWS SECRET: There is no one-size-fits-all method for potty training.

That's not to say there aren't good resources and ideas out there that can help your potty-training effort; there are plenty. Sifting through all the advice . . . from "experts," well-meaning family members, or any other of a number of sources, can be difficult. There's so much of it! And you definitely can't rely on the stories of any other kids to tell you how it will be for your child.

Potty training happens in stages. First, there's day training, when a child is diaper free during the day and doing just fine. Night training comes later. Some kids do great during the day for a very long time, but for that same long time still need a diaper at night, while other kids master control in both situations very quickly.

SHEKNOWS SECRET: The waterproof mattress pad on your child's bed will be your favorite piece of baby gear for a while.

Have I Mentioned All Kids Are Different Yet?

As you start to think about potty training, you might hear adages brought up as if they are fact: "Everyone knows it's easier to potty train girls than boys" or "This is the right way to potty train a child" and other such ridiculousness.

"I feel a little guilty about how easy potty training was in our house. My children were at a wonderful daycare at the time, and their caregivers took the initiative and did most of that work." —Jen O.

Add to it all that each gender has different equipment—and possibly different issues with that equipment—and it's another reminder that every kid is different. One gender isn't "easier" than the other, they are just different. I personally think that boys can be easier to train—especially if it's a warmer climate and/or a warm season. I've never known a little boy who hasn't loved to pee in the woods, or in the shrubs in front of the house. It doesn't hold quite the same allure for the little girls.

Goal Setting

Setting goals during potty training can be very effective in encouraging a child to think about the feelings he is having in the lower abdomen and acting on what they mean. But the reward for reaching the goal has to be something they really want, something with real appeal—a doll, truck, afternoon with just you to get ice cream sundaes. To that end, to track the progress of that goal, more than a few moms have broken out the proverbial sticker chart.

If I never see another sticker chart, I will be a happy mom. Sure, they were useful for some of my kids' behaviors over the years, but we had some moments during potty training when it seemed all I did was manage stickers. Stickers in the morning, stickers in the evening, stickers in the middle of the night. My son learned that if he just sat on the potty he'd get a sticker—whether he really tried to go or not. Eventually I figured out that my son had figured out how to manipulate me (because I hadn't been precise enough in declaring the rules for rewarding with stickers). I felt a little dumb and threw that sticker chart in the recycling.

SHEKNOWS SECRET: If you use a sticker chart, be very clear about your expectations and about what circumstances lead to a sticker.

Obviously, you must be very clear in your expectations if you go this route; it's not just what constitutes a try or an accident. How many days without accidents, and what constitutes an accident? Do they have to be consecutive days? And what, exactly, is the reward?

"My youngest liked to be naked, but I liked my carpets and upholstery, so he could only be naked after going to the potty. He would potty, strip down, and run up and down the hallway as we yelled, 'Naked, naked, naked!' Thus, the Naked Fun Run was born." —Ellen S.

No Punishing over the Potty

Since potty training is one of those skills that kids will eventually master, it's important that both you and your child remember that, every day. It's reassuring for both of you, and maybe can help you avoid reacting punitively to accidents and backsliding. One of the last things you want is for your child to associate the potty with punishment. As a parent, cleaning up some of those accidents can be quite disgusting and put you in a less-than-stellar mood, but punishment and shame associated with using the potty is difficult to turn around. Your child is already pretty embarrassed about the accident; wouldn't you be? Your child needs reassurance and problem solving to help prevent it from happening again, not punishment.

SHEKNOWS SECRET: You don't want your child to associate the potty with punishment.

Forward, Backward

Two steps forward, one step back. One step forward, three steps back. Four steps forward, one step back. Potty training can be like that—no expected rhythm to progress, and always a little uncertainty.

Accidents are one thing, but regression is another. If your child has been doing great on the potty for weeks but all of a sudden is having accident after accident, it may not be about potty training at all. It may be about some other stress in her life, something she's nervous about or scared of. If, for example, your child has been told she can't go to preschool unless she is in underwear, maybe she's scared of preschool and this is her way to make sure she doesn't go? Again, instead of punishing look at the bigger picture. Is something else going on?

SHEKNOWS SECRET: A sudden regression in potty training may indicate the child is stressed over something else in her life.

Regressions can also have their source in physical circumstances. If something with your child's lower plumbing doesn't feel quite right, or a bowel movement hurts, your daughter may simply decide to stop pooping. If you can't quite convince your child to go again on her own, seek professional help. You child's pediatrician probably has a few tricks and tips hidden away (as well as the ability to recognize any other potential issues), and sometimes just hearing from a different respected adult can convince a child to give it a go again.

Sometimes Diapers Are Easier

Remember when you went on that road trip in college? After holding your bladder for hours, you finally had to use a nasty truck stop restroom. You managed to find relief without touching anything and vowed never to return to such a disgusting place. Guess what? You're going back there, with your child, and it's going to be even worse.

"Consistency is key. Once you make the decision to potty train and your child is showing signs of readiness, stick to it and REMAIN CALM. It can be very frustrating (for all parties included) during the training process, but the cooler and more enthusiastic you stay about it, the better your child will do." —Chyler Leigh

At some point during potty training and just after initial potty training success, you'll be out and about and your child is going to say to you, "Mommy, I gotta go. Now." You will have to drop everything and find the closest restroom, and it will be foul.

The contortions you will go through to get your child relief without having him touch anything (and you touching anything only minimally) will be extraordinary. You will impress even yourself. You will pull muscles before you'll let your child touch anything. And you will make it through that experience and celebrate by pretty much dousing yourself and your son with antibacterial hand gel.

Then you will say to yourself, "A diaper would have been so much easier than this." Yeah, it would have.

"You may want to think twice before you throw Cheerios into the potty to give your son something to 'aim at' when learning to pee-pee. Apparently mistaking the toilet bowl for his cereal bowl, my son was busted eating Cheerios out of the potty. Let's just say we didn't try that technique again!" —Kim G.

As wonderful an achievement as potty training is for your child, until it is *very* firmly established, it can be a major pain in the patootie. It's a pain for you because of the sheer stress of pre-emptive potty planning, and it's a pain for your child if he gets stressed out and holds it in too long, thereby having an accident or becoming constipated. What fun.

Underwear All the Time

Like dealing with a sleep routine, complete, final, and secure potty training is a process, not a single event. You'll see that light at the end of the tunnel long before you'll actually make it there, and even when you realize you are there, it can be a surprise. A pleasant one, of course, but a surprise. You may spend several weeks pinching yourself: "Are we really all set?"

SHEKNOWS SECRET: Like waiting for your baby to sleep through the night, you'll see potty training progress little by little.

The other side of potty training is really a wonderful thing. It may take some time to get there, but keep at it. It will be an achievement both you and your child will be proud of. Along the way, though, buy some extra antibacterial hand gel. You'll be needing it.

CHAPTER 16

Every Child Is a Genius, Not Just Yours

C'mon, admit it. You've watched your child do this or that and thought to yourself, "She's so smart! She's a genius!" She's smart and perfect in your eyes, but is she really a perfect child, a genius? Well . . . probably not.

Of course your children are great and awesome, because they are your kids and you love them so much, and that's just how it should be. Your kids deserve that level of love and support—heck, adoration—from you. Every child deserves to be championed and cheered and it is our great responsibility and privilege as moms to do that. You *should* be proud of their accomplishments—but above all, let them be kids!

Get Out the Pom-Poms!

One of the most fun things about being a parent is being your child's cheerleader. Encouraging your child to try new things and seeing success, from taking that first step to riding a bicycle for the first time, from identifying a letter for the first time to reading a word, from being a shy toddler to an outgoing almost-kindergartener, each day is filled with the opportunity to encourage and support and cheer. Even the moms who smirked at and ridiculed the cheerleaders in high school and vowed they would never be like that find themselves a child's personal cheerleader. Thankfully, you don't have to be remotely perky to fill this role perfectly.

As a parent, it's so exciting to see your child succeed. It's not just a smile, but also a deep-gut feeling of pride that makes you feel so full you think you might burst. And it's not just pride in your child, it's pride in yourself—a moment when you realize maybe you're doing some of this parenting thing right! It's an ego boost for both of you, as it should be.

"Parents of young children should realize that few people, and maybe no one, will find their children as enchanting as they do." —Barbara Walters

Being your child's personal cheerleader is also difficult at times. Sometimes being a cheerleader means supporting them when they fail or when things don't go as planned. Yes, sometimes you have to watch your kids fail. That feeling that was meant to be pride can now feel like it's going to break your heart having to watch your child experience disappointment. When they just can't get the hang of that bicycle or the swing or the reading or the math, or just about anything, the frustration builds. That's when the cheerleading job gets harder and even more critically important, when you're trying to encourage them in the face of something less than success.

Cheerleader or Helicopter?

When we are our children's cheerleaders, it can be an easy segue to helicopter parenting. Often, we don't realize we are doing it. I don't know a single mom who wants to be a helicopter parent, yet I know many moms who admit they have crossed over that line now and again, or even often. But what really defines a helicopter parent can be nebulous, difficult to discern, and it's a little different for every parent.

SHEKNOWS SECRET: Kids need to fail sometimes to learn how to succeed.

Kids do need to fail somewhere along the way. They need to fall off the bike before they can master balance; they need to make some mistakes to be able to really learn about doing things right. That's not to say they need to fail all the time, but they need to learn on their own as much as we teach them. When parenting crosses the invisible line and doesn't allow these important life lessons, it may be crossing into helicopter parenting.

Finding a Balance with Praise

While there is still some debate about this, there's a school of thought that says overpraise can be just as problematic as not enough praise. Too much praise and your child thinks he can do no wrong; not enough and he thinks he can do no right. With this in mind, cheerleading becomes less absolute and more situational and specific.

See Your Whole Child

It's difficult to recognize that your children are less than perfect and won't succeed at everything they try the first time. We want so much for our kids, and we want to see the best. Sometimes only seeing the best hides reality and makes reality hit even harder when it does come through, eventually.

SHEKNOWS SECRET: Your child is not perfect, and you are not a perfect parent. But you are perfect for each other.

In some ways, we know our children too well. We become accustomed to their habits and idiosyncrasies, and we tend to understand their personalities. It's easy for us to overlook the not-so-perfect parts of our children, and even deny they exist. We accommodate their quirks while not even realizing we are doing it.

Seeing the Big Development Picture

It's easy to get caught up in the day to day with our children. It's natural; it's our job! But it's also important to try to see the big picture.

During the preschool years, when our children are emerging more and more into their own selves, is when possible bigger-picture issues might start to be more apparent. It's behavioral issues, yes, but it's also when developmental milestones can be less precise. Specific behaviors may or may not be a part of that.

> *"Where parents do too much for their children, the children will not do much for themselves."*
> *—Elbert Hubbard*

When your child was an infant, there were definite milestones at specific months—certain fine and gross motor skills at certain ages in weeks or months. As kids get into the preschool years, some developmental milestones can be more subtle or partially met or a child can learn to compensate in other ways. When you look at a group of kids with essentially the same chronological age, each one can be completely normal in and of themselves and within the group, but the developmental range they display can be vast. It can be hard to tell when something—a behavior or a response—is within the range of normal or just beyond it.

At the same time, because you know your kid so well, you make accommodations to his developmental age and stage as you go along. For example, you may have adjusted your responses to his temper because, of course, you are with him so much and really don't know differently. It's easier to go with the flow, easier to avoid addressing some underlying behavior. Of course it feels normal to you, it's your everyday life! Similarly, for example, you may be so used to your child's speech that you are not able to hear that he's having real difficulty saying Rs and Ss.

SHEKNOWS SECRET: Trust your mommy instinct when it comes to your child's developmental milestones. It knows things you may not think you know.

Straight comparison to other kids isn't quite appropriate in development and behavior, but neither is looking at your child in a vacuum. If there's something not quite right happening with your child, something a little off that you can't identify, listen to your gut instinct. You have a mommy instinct deep inside you, and it knows things you may not think you know. Listen to it.

SHEKNOWS HOW TO COPE WITH AUTISM

Finding out that your child has autism can be devastating news, but rarely is the situation as dire as you might expect. Contrary to some common beliefs, many kids with autism can smile, make eye contact, play, and cuddle! Now there are also more opportunities than ever for children with autism to grow up and be productive members of society . . . and many believe that some of these amazing people who see things in their own unique way will change the world for the better. (According to many researchers, Albert Einstein, Thomas Jefferson, and Sir Isaac Newton may well have been on the autistic spectrum.) For more information on autism, go to *www.SheKnows.com/autism.*

It's Okay to Let Go of Some Dreams

We all have hopes and dreams for our children. They started when they were still rice-sized miracles implanted into the wall of our uteruses. Our children may fulfill these dreams, or they may not. Your child, perfect in your eyes, may not be perfect.

Your three- or four-year-old child may be perfectly delightful with adults in many situations, but really struggle in social interactions with other children her age. She may have perfect fine-motor skills for picking up her food, but may have a quirky gait when she tries to run. She may love drawing but have difficulty recognizing patterns and figures. She may get overwhelmed trying to manage a request with more than one step.

"My natural tendency is to be a helicopter parent, but I force myself to resist this inclination, or at least hide it from the children. I'm the mother who lets her four-year-old go over to play in the neighbor children's yard, then runs out every ten minutes and hides in the bushes to check on him." —Mary Lou B.

Admitting that your perfect child is something less than absolutely perfect—and in fact may need a little boost to help her along—can be a very emotional step. You can feel like you've done something wrong or it can feel like grief. It's all wrapped up in what we hope for them and what we hope for ourselves. And like other manifestations of grief, you can experience denial, anger, deep sadness, and bargaining on your way to acceptance and action.

But Don't Go Looking for Trouble

All that said, as your child develops and grows, don't go looking for trouble where there is none. Maybe an outburst or inappropriate behavior at preschool was just a bad day and a good talk will resolve it. Not every funny gait needs a diagnosis; maybe your child just needs a few months after a growth spurt to recoordinate his limbs. Maybe that developmental point at which your son recognizes patterns will switch on next week. Maybe he is appropriately social with other kids, but you just haven't seen it.

Again, listen to your mommy instinct. We have it for a reason! Ask close friends their opinions, if you must, but also recognize that even if your child is less than perfect, sometimes a quirk is just a quirk and that's okay.

Forget Teaching Moments and Just Have Fun

As you think about your child's successes and dreams, it's difficult not to also think about how much and how well she is learning. We've all heard the refrain dozens of times: You are your child's first teacher. You are the one who introduces them to learning and teaches them the basics of both book learning and life learning, whether it's saying "please" and "thank you" or which color is green or counting to ten. You teach it all.

You probably do this mostly without thought. You don't typically wake up in the morning and think, "Today I will teach my daughter about the letter 'G'" or "I think early math skills are on the learning plan for my daughter today." Well, maybe some of us do, but for the most part, the teaching we do is instinctual and comfortable and fun and a part of regular parenting.

Your daughter asks a question and you answer. That's teaching. You notice her trying to figure out how and why a toy works the way it does. You show her, explain to her. That's teaching. You live your everyday life. That's teaching.

Learning the Easy Way

Parenting can be hard work, but it can also be great fun. And the preschool-aged child is a heck of a lot of fun.

"My children's brilliance, open hearts, and excitement with the natural world bring me joy. Their ability to contextualize at a young age always blew me away, how they put it all together!"

—Kellie B.

He can be a great companion, too. A couple of years ago a trip to the zoo would have been fun, but he probably became too tired after just an hour or so. Now you could go and really see the animals, ask questions, and talk about them! He enjoys trips to the library to pick out books, and has probably developed a favorite category of toy.

SHEKNOWS SECRET: If you haven't done much traveling with your child, try it now.

It's probably easier to travel with your child at this age, too. Try museums, hikes, sporting events. You will be amazed at what he is capable of at this age. He truly is a blast. And he's learning from you every minute, but don't let that scare you.

Research Overload

In our media-saturated culture, you can't go a day without hearing about some new study that declares something about the way children learn or develop. While such research was likely happening just as often years ago, the Internet brings it all into our homes sooner, and in tidy sound bites (which may or may not be exactly accurate). We are inundated with information about the right and wrong way to do things, at least this week. It could change next week with the next round of new research released.

This kind of intense release of findings and theories can be both good and less than ideal. It's really terrific that we have a better understanding of how early play with shapes helps develop both reading and math skills or how morals and empathy develop and all that; it can help focus our energies and help us refine parenting. If, that is, we can sort out what it all means. Such details can also distract us from the job of parenting.

So much of this research has focused on how kids learn, and that's a good thing overall. Studies back up the basic premise that kids learn through play. Of course they do! Moms could accurately have declared this through observation and commonsense decades, if not centuries, ago.

> *"My younger daughters are still good friends with the kids they met at preschool, so I suspect they have created their own memories with their friends, which is great." —Debby S.*

This research has a downside, however. Keeping studies about the exact mechanisms of how kids learn in the forefront of the media for a few years has pushed us toward thinking inordinately about teaching moments and whether certain toys—toys!—are appropriately educational. Confirmation of how kids learn through play has actually steered us away from truly free play. Not to mention the moneymaking opportunities of marketing to nervous parents who want to do the best for their children.

Resource Overload

In spite of the prevalence of online shopping, they still come in the mail: the educational toy catalogs. Some are thick and some are thin, some are trying to sell the latest invention while some tout a return to "old fashioned" with specific materials and nonelectronic technology. Some engage all the current trends: learning, old-time materials, contemporary design, and environmentally friendly. Some are pricey and some are even more pricey.

Put Down the Flash Cards!

As much as our children have the capacity to learn through play, not every moment has to be a teaching moment or one with just the right educational toy. Not every moment is about taking advantage of that learning capacity and adding some foundational concept. Sometimes you just need to let go, have fun, and let your child have fun.

SHEKNOWS SECRET: You can let your child play without having an educational goal in mind.

Yes, some kids do like flash cards. I wouldn't say I've met any of them, but I understand they do exist. If it's the only choice in the room, then maybe my kids would have played with flash cards, too, but it's so much more fun for both of us to watch the kids create elaborate scenes with plastic figures and their accessories, to see what their imaginations create.

"I think, at a child's birth, if a mother could ask a fairy godmother to endow it with the most useful gift, that gift should be curiosity." —Eleanor Roosevelt

I've watched my kids create fantastic buildings, impossibly complicated train tracks, imagine crazy plots, and spend what seemed like hours to them (really five minutes or so) trying to figure out how something worked. I've also watched them dance to the radio when they thought no one was watching (and even when they did) and stare off into space and daydream. Those were happy moments.

Better yet, I've sat down on the floor with my kids and taken direction about where the next horse goes, eaten millions of imaginary meals, held those impossible train tracks together for just one engine trip, and sipped lemonade with my pinky out during a living room tea party.

> *"My husband used to spend hours sitting on the back porch with our preschool son looking at the night sky and talking about the stars and constellations."*
> —*Jen O.*

I've even taught—when asked. After overhearing her brother talking about multiplication tables from his homework, my daughter asked me what five times three meant. I explained it—briefly—using plastic figures from her play set: five knights in one grouping, five sea creatures in another, and five vehicles in still another. We added them all up, then rearranged them in five groups of three, added them up again, then she went back to the scene she'd created using princesses and an airport. The idea of allowing children to learn through play doesn't preclude teaching moments, but it doesn't force them either. Teach when asked, but understand it's okay if you're not asked. Sometimes play is just about fun and bonding.

Give yourself and your child time to let go. Taking teaching moments when they present themselves or encouraging educational toys is not a bad thing, but it's not all there is. Likewise, not taking the lead on those potential teaching moments or leaving the educational toys in the toy bin is not a bad thing either. Sometimes you just need a break from all that, and your child probably does, too.

SHEKNOWS CRAFTY KIDS

Most kids are natural-born artists, and love to paint, draw, and decorate. Luckily, to encourage their creativity, you don't need to spend much (if any) money! Start with something as simple as a cardboard box, then give your child some crayons, pens, or paint. Alternatively, provide your kids with glue and send them outside to find leaves and pinecones, pebbles, and sand to decorate their box. Give them ideas and encouragement, but let the choices and craftiness be their own! Find many more craft ideas at *http://SheKnows .com/articles/family-fun/family-activities.htm.*

Enjoy Your Child

Doesn't it seem like yesterday that your baby was born? And now she is a walking, talking, funny little person that you can't imagine not having had in your life. It went so fast, didn't it? You blinked, and suddenly you were here. Blink again and she might be a teenager, blink one more time and she might be graduating from college.

It can be easy to get caught up in the research and the shoulds and the preparing for this or that; media pushes it, and we push it on ourselves. It can be easy to get distracted from an essential part of your life together: enjoying each other.

EPILOGUE

The Bus Pulls Away

Flash forward fourteen years. It's a sunny September morning, the first day of school. And when I say "flash," I mean it. How did I get to be a forty-something mother of three with all the attendant joy, stress, and experience that goes along with that?

My first baby, now thirteen, will be taller than me by Christmas (and I'm not short). His adolescent self is just as wonderful and challenging as his toddler self was. He's a great kid.

My second baby is nine. His mischievous grin, wacky sense of humor, and impetuous manner remind me of my father's curse to me: "I hope you have a child just like you!" He's also a great kid.

My third baby—my last baby—is five. In a few minutes, she will climb aboard the bus for her first day of kindergarten. My heart is bursting with pride at how ready she is to go, my head is thrilled for all the learning and fun to come, and my eyes are heavy with tears. My baby is taking another step away from me. I take deep breaths, trying to maintain composure.

When did my family get to be so . . . big? Not numbers big, but physically big. And how is this heart that loves them so much still contained in a single human body?

On a day like today, past and future seem to come into view simultaneously. I see our past, though I can no longer grasp it; the future is coming closer, but still out of reach. I see my children stepping further and further away from me, and doing so with astonishing confidence. They still look to me, still need me, still rush back every now and again, but it's two steps forward, one step back—then two steps forward again.

I know, as bittersweet as it is, that this is what is supposed to happen. My job, from the moment my children were born, was not only to love and protect them, but also to teach them how to leave; to teach them how to be productive, confident, capable members of society. If I do my job right—and it's a big if—they will not need me at some point. They will want me, and I will be there gladly, but they will not need me. It turns out that as a parent my biggest job is to plan my obsolescence. Ouch.

Every day marks another step toward my children leaving me, this waiting for the kindergarten bus included. The minutes tick by. We talk and laugh, but my inner voice is as loud as anything physically around me. I wonder, "Did I get it right? Did we laugh enough? Does she have enough happy memories of these early years? Did I do right by her? By her brothers before her? And how will I ever really know?"

When I think about the almost decade and a half since I first knew I'd be a mother, I remember some very long days, yet their cumulative total seems to have passed in a blink of an eye. We have achieved so much, had so much fun, felt every emotion from joy to despair, endured what we never knew we could endure, and wanted more.

There is still much more to come. This momentous event, getting on the big yellow bus, is another step on a much greater journey for all of us. I'm not obsolete quite yet.

Too soon, there's the rumbling of the bus over the hill and the squeak of the brakes as it slows and stops. My daughter is giddy.

She's bouncing while hugging my leg. My husband and I each reach down to give her hugs and kisses and I love yous and have funs and one more hug and kiss.

She steps on the bus. She turns and waves. "Bye, Mama!" I take a picture, tears no longer contained. I see her sit next to a new friend as the doors fold shut. She waves, with a big grin on her face. The bus starts to accelerate.

There she goes.

APPENDIX

Resources

While by no means comprehensive, the following Internet sites can provide resources during pregnancy and early childhood.

General Information and Support

- SheKnows: *www.SheKnows.com*
Getting to the heart of what it really means to be a woman, SheKnows' editors are dedicated to providing daily content for women seeking advice, information, and a fresh, fun take on life. The SheKnows audience gains access to exclusive content on parenting, health and wellness, relationships, beauty and style, and more, and are offered a stimulating, well-rounded online experience enhanced with a vibrant message board community, free games and activities, and captivating blogs.

Health and Development

- American Academy of Pediatrics: *www.aap.org*
- American College of Obstetricians and Gynecologists: *www.acog.org*

- Asthma and Allergy Foundation of America: *www.aafa.org*
- Centers for Disease Control and Prevention Learn the Signs site: *www.cdc.gov/ncbddd/actearly/index.html*
- Doulas of North America: *www.dona.org*
- Food Allergy and Anaphylaxis Network: *www.faan.org*
- International Lactation Consultant Association: *www.ilca.org*
- La Leche League: *www.llli.org*
- National Association of Certified Professional Midwives: *www.nacpm.org*
- National Sleep Foundation: *www.nsf.org*
- North American Registry of Midwives: *www.narm.org*

Child Safety and Education

- Children's Safety Network: *www.childrenssafetynetwork.org*
- Consumer Product Safety Commission: *www.cpsc.gov*
- Early Childhood Education at the Department of Education: *www.ed.gov/parents/earlychild/ready/resources.html*
- National Association for the Education of Young Children: *www.naeyc.org*

Pregnancy, Family, and Employment Law

Many laws pertaining to pregnancy, family, and employment vary by state. See your state's government website for state-specific information. Additional information can be found at:

- Equal Employment Opportunity Commission: *www.eeoc.gov*
- United States Department of Labor: *www.dol.gov*

Academic Research Institutions

Numerous academic institutions around the country maintain divisions and departments devoted to the study and understanding of child development. These groups can be tremendous resources for information and reassurance.

- New York University Child Study Center: *www.aboutourkids .org*
- University of California at Berkeley Institute of Human Development: *www.ihd.berkeley.edu/child.htm*
- University of Virginia Child Study Center: *www.faculty .virginia.edu/childstudycenter*
- Yale University Child Study Center: *www.childstudycenter .yale.edu*

Index

through the night, 109–11
training *vs.* learning,
114–16
Soothing (sleep method), 113
Spock, Benjamin, 62
Spoiling, concerns about,
71–72
Spouses/partners, 121–32
birth plan and, 50, 51
communicating with,
124–25
coparenting with, 128–29
dating, 129–30
discipline and, 172–73
family time and, 130–31
loyalties *vs.* priorities,
123–25
mutual compassion, 127
parenting goals and biases,
125–27
setting priorities, 122–23
Sticker charts, 181–82
Stretch marks, 27–29

tantrums in, 165–66
Traveling with children, 195

V
Vaccines, 91
Van Gogh, Vincent, 69
VBAC, 47
Vitamins, prenatal, 19

W
Walters, Barbara, 188
Waterbirth, 44
Weight. *See also* Diet and
nutrition (mother)
breastfeeding and, 94
losing post-pregnancy,
79–81
during pregnancy, 23–24
Weisz, Rachel, 77

T
Tantrums, 165–66
Terrible twos. *See* Toddlers
Toddlers, 162–75
emerging personality/
independence in,
162–63
managing expectations,
164–65

Printed in the United States
By Bookmasters